Playful Quilts for Kids

Carolyn Vosburg Hall

Published by

700 East State Street • Iola, WI 54990-0001
715-445-2214 • 888-457-2873

Our toll-free number to place an order or obtain
a free catalog is (800) 258-0929.

Library of Congress Catalog Number: 2004107430

ISBN: 0-87349-809-7

Designed by Marilyn McGrane

Edited by Susan Sliwicki

Printed in The United States of America

Table of Contents

Introduction

When is a quilt more than a quilt? When it also is a game, a costume, a toy or a learning tool. Life is livelier when the things used every day are colorful, fun and inventive.

Here are 20 projects that are more than quilts. Kids can ride or wear them, use them to learn the alphabet, practice working buttonholes, change them into something else or cuddle under them for naps. Each quilt project comes with suggestions for ways to play with it, and inventive kids will come up with plenty of ideas on their own.

Many of these quilts, such as the Bumper Car Quilt, are based on childhood games. My sister or I would sit at the top of the stairs on an old, gray wool blanket, pull it up over our feet and go "bump, bump, bump" down the whole flight. The Dragon Quilt idea came from the same old blanket.

Why make quilts for kids? We moms, grandmas, aunts and others stitch our memories and our affection into every quilt we make. No quilts remain that I made for my now-adult children. They have been loved to tatters, and so will yours.

Not all quilts are quilted. Not all quilted things are quilts. This book has both. A traditional quilt (noun) has a pieced front in a geometric pattern, a backing fabric and a layer of filler in between. All three layers are joined together with hand or machine topstitching at close intervals. Quilt (as a verb) means to sew layers together to achieve puffiness. You can do this on pillows, games, blankets or costumes to delightful effect. Both kinds of quilting make good children's quilts.

The bed in most children's rooms is the biggest, most visible surface. This is a perfect place for a kid's quilt to serve as an art object or a plaything. This can set the tone and decor for the entire room. And don't forget the walls. A few of these quilts are meant as wall hangings, both as decorative features and games. These have rod pockets sewn in to facilitate display. It's a good idea to hang the ones with pockets low enough for children to pop stuffed toys in and out.

Several patterns are designed with shortcuts to assure that you can finish the quilt before the child grows up. They have backgrounds of single-layer fleece, use double-sided, pre-quilted fabrics or feature puffy, faux fur. These ideas shorten or eliminate time-consuming quilting of the layers.

Dedication

This book is dedicated to generations of quilt makers in my family: my mom, Doris Vosburg; my sister, Lois Goodrich; my daughter, Claudia Stroud; and my granddaughter, Hattie Stroud.

Acknowledgments

Thanks to project helpers Ross Hall, Briana and Brent Hood, Sandy Hall, Emily and Ian Goodrich and Michael, Sean and Kyle Goodrich.

Getting Started

A major part of making a quilt is selecting the fabrics for it. The main guide in choosing fabrics is finding the right combination of colors, and equally important, the right characteristic of fabrics.

CHAPTER
1

Choosing Fabrics

Choosing fabrics primarily for color works best on projects that won't be washed, such as wall hangings. Those pieces will need only dusting or vacuuming now and then. But select washable, long-wear fabrics for toys that will take a lot of loving.

Each project lists the kinds of fabrics used, why they suit the project and other choices you can make. For example, the ABC Quilt pockets need a sturdy fabric for machine-embroidered letters, the Wizard Cape works best in a swirling, lightweight fabric, and the Mitten Quilt makes a fine sleeping bag in a soft, stretchy fleece.

Be guided by the colors and fabrics shown, or select your own assortment of fabrics with similar characteristics. It is more important that the colors of a project all look good together than that all colors match exactly those used on the projects in this book. If you choose to vary the colors, lay them all together to see how they harmonize.

Fabrics used in these kids' quilts are easy to find and affordable. Nearly all were found in local stores. Some of the smaller pieces came from my stash of fabrics saved over the years.

It helps to read the hangtags when you buy the fabric. For example, children's clothing fabrics should be nonflammable for safety's sake. People more organized than I pin labels that tell content and care data onto the fabrics in their collections. Lacking a label, I end up touching a hot iron to a sample to see if it fries. You can run a piece of unknown fabric through a washing and drying cycle to see how it holds up. Some fabrics, such as cottons, need preshrinking, and some will lose the filler added to give better stability.

Fleece Fabric

Half of the projects in this book call for fleece, a fairly recent entry into the home sewer's fabric stash. A New England man developed it by recycling plastic bottles into fibers.

Fleece is wonderful fabric that is fluffy, warm, nonfraying and easy to use. It is ideal for a lot of kids' stuff, but it does need some special care.

Kinds of Fleece

Fleece comes in several kinds and grades, and usually is sold in 60" widths. Top-grade fleece, as

A large fabric stash is a sign of a seasoned quilter or sewer.

marked on the hangtags of the fabric bolts, will not pill with use. If your fleece pills with use, you can brush it to restore the nap.

Some fleece has a brushed surface on one side only and a smooth double-knit on the other. Early on, most fleece prints were quite sporty, because they were used for outerwear where the brushed finish results in a soft, fuzzy design. Fleece now is appearing in an ever-widening range of colors and designs.

Washing Fleece

You can wash fleece in the washing machine. If fleece is very wrinkled, prewash it and dry in a cool to warm dryer. General recommendations are to use a powdered detergent to remove dirt, because liquid detergents simply coat the fleece fabric.

Pressing Fleece

Ironing fleece must be done carefully, if at all. Since it is made of plastic, it will melt under a hot iron. Direct contact with a heated iron can emboss a permanent imprint on fleece. If you plan to appliqué on fleece, use a steam cloth over

Fleece.

use Steam-a-Seam™, which is a pressure-sensitive adhesive, to keep the appliqué in place for sewing.

Sewing Fleece

Fleece is knitted and then brushed to raise a nap on the surface. There *is* a right side to fleece, although it may not matter to your project. To determine the right side, check which way the fabric curls along a cut edge when stretched. Cut fleece curls to the wrong side. This stretchy, knit fabric does not fray when cut, so you need not hem edges, nor overcast or bind seams.

Flexible fleece is quite easy to sew by machine. However, it is best to place pins across the stitch line to keep the sides even and prevent the fabric from stretching. Avoid damaging the cutter when serging fleece by placing pins 3" from the edge. You will need to set the differential feed when you serge the fleece to prevent it from stretching out of shape.

Thick fleece can challenge your sewing machine, so avoid sewing too many layers at once. Very narrow seams also may be difficult to machine sew because the fleece is lofty. It may stick in the presser foot or drag off the seam line. Use a tool, such as a long pin, to flatten the edge as it feeds into the machine.

Embroidering Fleece

If you machine embroider on fleece, you will need tear-away backing so it will not stretch out of shape. The backing will show on the reverse side, so plan to line the quilt. When satin stitching or appliquéing, lengthen the zigzag stitch setting for a less solid line so it won't pucker.

Cotton and Cotton-Polyester Fabric

Cotton fabrics made for quilting are used on many of the projects. Cotton or cotton-polyester mixes wash well, are soft yet tightly woven, come in an array of prints and colors, and sew well by hand or machine.

These lightweight fabrics require added volume, such as stuffing, filler or added layers, to make good quilts. Satin stitching or machine embroidery on lightweight cotton fabric needs backing stabilizer to keep it from puckering. Woven cottons need their edges hemmed or finished because they will fray.

Cotton or cotton-polyester mixes come in other forms. The Scrambled People and ABC quilts use a heavy, duck cloth cotton fabric. This canvas-like fabric provides its own stability, and, as a rule, machine satin stitching does not stretch or pucker it. This is a good choice for machine embroidery. Even so, the individual threads, which are larger than quilting cottons, can make small details harder to sew, such as turned corners. To do this, you will need to take two tiny machine sewn stitches angled across a corner seam, then clip and grade the seam allowance so it fits within the turned corner.

Polyester Fabric

Silky polyester fabric is recommended in several projects, such as the Wizard Cape, for its special qualities. Its fabric is washable, sturdy, satiny and lightweight. Not only does the surface have a satin sheen, but also the fabric drapes softly and usually does not wrinkle.

These qualities make sewing more of a challenge, because silky

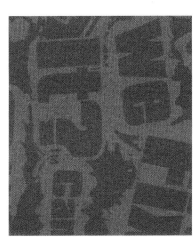

Cotton fabric.

Cotton-polyester blend fabric.

Polyester fabric.

fabric will slip, slide and maybe even pucker when being sewn or cut into pattern shapes. But don't worry. You can measure and cut the patterns on a large, flat surface using pins to secure layers. Use sharp scissors or a rotary cutter along with a metal yardstick for straight seams. Even better, cut pieces singly.

When machine sewing, secure seams with quilting pins across the seam lines, and guide polyester fabric carefully.

Faux Fur

Faux fur is used for the Bear Hugger, the Dog Pillow and other projects. Faux fur usually is knitted on the backside so it does not ravel, and it has various lengths of nap on the face.

Some early faux furs matted with use, but current faux furs are realistic looking, washable and wear well. The Bear Hugger quilt you see pictured has been through the laundry after a play session with my granddaughter, and it still looks like new. Tips on sewing fur are given in that project.

Novelty Fabrics

Novelty fabrics appear in several projects. These include the silver-embossed dancer's dress in the Scrambled People Quilt and the nonwoven felt flowers in the Flower Button Quilt.

The Circus Train Wall Hanging calls for clear vinyl, which makes the toys in the wagons visible. Sewing this material requires tear-away backing so the vinyl won't stick on the needle plate or the presser foot; instructions are provided. Ribbons, tissue-thin metallic fabrics and gold roping that is hot glued in place also are used in this wall hanging project. For a washable quilt, substitute sturdy fabrics and sew, rather than glue, embellishments.

Seasonal Fabrics

Can't find the fabric used for the project you've chosen to make? No surprise. I regularly roam the fabric store aisles searching for just the right ones. Many fabrics are seasonal, such as faux furs in the fall for stuffed toys, glittery metallic fabrics for the holiday season, and pastel cotton colors for spring.

Many of the fabrics used in these projects came from my lifelong stash. I've collected material forever, buying a few yards of this or that gorgeous fabric just because I love it, or saving extra fabric from a project. If you can find the space, build up your own stash of fun fabrics.

Seasonal fabric.

Seasonal fabric.

Faux fur.

Felt.

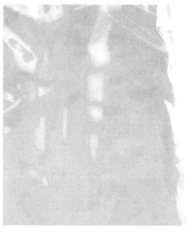
Vinyl.

Techniques and Tips

Using Patterns

Trace or photocopy patterns provided in this book to avoid cutting up the book and losing the backs of other pages. Each project will list what pattern pieces are needed. Occasionally, you will need to create templates or tear-away pattern pieces. When that occurs, special directions will be given.

Use a pencil — ink smears — to trace around the patterns on the backside of the fabric. Seam allowances measure about ¼" to provide a well-defined seam line.

While all of the patterns are full size and ready to use, several pattern pieces are given "on the fold" to save space in this book. It is best to make a full pattern piece of paper. To do this, trace the pattern with pins on the folded edge. Flip over the pattern to reverse it and trace the other side. You can skip the paper pattern and use this same technique on fabric. Cut it out carefully.

Cutting

Cutting fabrics requires sharp scissors or cutting blades. Mark the pattern on the fabric with pencil or chalk, then cut on the line.

Pinned pattern pieces may shift, so cut most fabrics singly, especially furs. To cut furs, slip the scissors tips through the nap and snip, snip, snip.

Long strips or blocks of fabric with straight sides can be cut using a metal ruler and rotary cutter with a pad underneath. Many fabrics will tear straight along the grain line for the most even edges.

No matter how accurate the pattern pieces look, I still draw seam lines on the back with a template pattern.

Sewing

Some fabrics require special techniques for sewing them, and instructions appear in the project directions. The three common techniques used are sewing machine stitching, from straight to satin stitching; serging, which trims off the seam allowances as it overcasts the edges; and hand sewing of one kind or another.

Threads used include cone threads for the serger, which offer a lot of sturdy thread for the money; hand quilting thread, which slides through the layers of fabric and doesn't tangle; lustrous machine embroidery thread, which makes machine embroidery shine; and clear monofilament thread, which is used for invisible seams.

Knots must be firmly tied on children's quilts because they need to withstand wear and tear. For example, the teething ring must be sewn firmly onto the Blankie quilt. To sew a knot, use a sturdy, knotted, double thread. Sew into the fabric and back, and then sew between the double threads to secure the first stitches. To the end, sew a loop next to the emerging thread, wrap the thread twice around the needle tip, and pull tightly to knot. Then sew a second knot the same way. To hide the ends, sew into the back side 1" to 2" away to embed the end, then clip off the thread at the fabric surface.

Finishing Touches

Stuffing And Batting

Stuffing has changed and improved through the ages. Teddy bears used to be stuffed with excelsior, or wood shavings, which eventually turned to sawdust.

Most stuffing now is polyester fiber called fiberfill. It is spun from synthetics extruded through a spinneret to make a monofilament line, and then it is chopped into shorter fibers. Fiberfill ranks as the No. 1 stuffing for toys. It is lightweight, safe, washable, easy to use and readily available. It doesn't shift much or decompose, either.

Different-shaped fibers have different qualities, such as high loft, permanent color and minimal cost. Some fiberfill quilt batting is bonded on the surface to require less quilting, and some has an adhesive surface to bond to the quilt face fabric.

Polystyrene pellets offer weighted, shifting filler, such as would be used in beanbags. Lacking this, use dried beans, lentils or popcorn.

Turning Small Toys

Turning small, sewn toys takes nimble fingers. To turn narrow parts, use a long, narrow tool such as a ¼" dowel, a wooden chopstick, bamboo skewer or the eraser end of a pencil.

Turn the narrow parts before turning the whole animal. Begin as close to the tip as possible, and work the piece onto the turning tool slowly and carefully. Don't let too much fabric bunch up.

For a really narrow part, lay a string inside the part before you sew it, then sew over the knotted end. Pull the string to turn the piece, but avoid allowing the fabric to bunch up too much. Then clip off the string. If a fabric just won't turn, settle for exposed seams on the narrow parts and trim close to the seam line.

Embellishments

An amazing variety of other materials can be used on kids' quilts. You'll see buttons, beads, ribbons, gold braid, toy eyes, hook and loop tape, zippers and squeeze paint. Methods to attach these items, such as sewing, tying or gluing, are given where needed.

Be cautious about adding buttons or other objects that a small child might swallow. Some embellishments also may limit how well a project washes and wears.

Other than that, have a great time making these projects any way you wish.

Baby Quilts

Quilts delight the five senses. Babies and moms can enjoy each day more when the things they commonly use stir their senses. Further, evidence proves that stimulated children learn more and learn faster. Babies are busy taking in the world with their eyes, fingers, noses, ears and tongues. Quilts give them textures to touch, such as fuzzy fur or soft fleece. There are colors and shapes to see and mom's voice to hear as she wraps her baby in a quilt. Chewing on a toy or a quilt binding gives babies a taste of the world. And a newly washed baby quilt gives off the smell of cleanness. Quilts you make can add so much to a child's life — and to yours. So here's to happy, smart babies.

CHAPTER

2

Bear Hugger

Materials

FABRIC
1 yd. of honey-color faux fur fabric, 60" wide with ½" pile

12" x 12" scrap of white faux fur fabric

5" x 5" scrap of brown suede cloth

6" x 6" scrap of backing fabric

BATTING
12" x 12" x 3" wad of fiberfill

NOTIONS
Threads in black, tan and white

TOOLS AND SUPPLIES
Pencil

1½" quilt pins

Sharp scissors

Sewing machine and/or hand sewing needle

This little quilt can be used as a changing pad for a small child or as a blankie for a toddler to drag around. The fur fabric used on both sides is a washable acrylic with ½" pile. You also can use outerwear fleece with a water-repellent fabric on one side for a washable changing pad.

Changing pads, towels, blankets — so many of the necessary items for tending babies need not be dull squares. Babies and moms can enjoy each day more when the things they commonly use are colorful, funny, inventive — whatever makes them happy.

This quilt was hand sewn, but it could just as well have been machine sewn. Details, such as the bear's features and paws, are machine appliquéd with a close zigzag stitch.

The fiberfill used in the bear's head serves as a thin pillow. Without the filler, the Hugger Bear flops more like a blanket.

Cut

YOU WILL NEED THE FOLLOWING PATTERN PIECES: Bear Body, Nose, Eyes, Feet Paws, Hand Paws

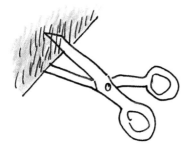

1. From the honey-colored faux fur cut two Bear Bodies. Use sharp scissors to cut a single layer from the reverse side, following the traced line.

TIP: When cutting faux fur, cut a single layer, make short snips with the scissors and slide the scissors tips under the fur pile to avoid snipping it off.

2. From the white faux fur cut two Feet Paws and two Hand Paws.

3. From the brown suede cut two Eyes and one Nose.

4. From the bonded filler cut a head-shaped piece to pad the Bear Hugger's head.

Appliqué

1. Position the Eye and Nose pieces on the Bear Hugger front.

2. Use 1½" quilting pins to pin Eye and Nose pieces. Pin across the stitch line to avoid hitting pins when sewing by machine

3. Set the machine to a wide satin stitch. Using black thread, appliqué these pieces onto the face. If the appliqué piece tends to shift, sew the edges first with a straight stitch, then zigzag over the stitch line.

4. Satin stitch the bear's mouth on the Bear Hugger front, using a backing fabric to stabilize it.

5. Align the Paw pieces on all four paws, then pin in place.

6. Switch to the white thread, and appliqué the paw pieces in place with a wide zigzag stitch. This stitching need not be as close as a satin stitch to hold just as well.

Fill

1. Add the bonded filling to the reverse side of the head.

2. Pin the filling in place with long quilting pins.

Sew

1. Align the Bear Body front and back pieces, right sides together, and pin across the seam line.

2. Sew the bear following a ¼" seam allowance. Leave a 6" opening at the tail area to turn the bear. Stitch the head filling in the seam as you join the Bear Hugger front and back.

TIP: The nap may get stuck in the seam, so brush it out of the seam line as you sew. Then use a long pin to pull fur pile out of the seam. Run the pin or a tool, such as a seam ripper, across any pile stuck in the seam to release it.

3. Turn the Bear Hugger fur side out. Poke all the seams out to completely turn the bear.

4. For the stuffed head, quilt the bear by hand stitching or topstitching across the chin line given on the pattern.

5. Hand sew the opening closed.

Blankie

Materials

FABRIC
½ yd. pastel green fleece
6" x 6" scrap of lime green fleece
7" x 7" scrap of light blue fleece
1" x 4" scrap of cream fleece
3" x 3" scrap of white fleece
2" x 3" scrap of gold fleece

NOTIONS
Packet of double 2" wide variegated-color blanket binding, or 5" x 72" polyester satin strip
Threads in orange, white and gold

EMBELLISHMENTS
Plastic teething ring
2" diameter blind-spot mirror
⅜" toy eye with post and washer

TOOLS AND SUPPLIES
Sharp scissors
Hand sewing needle
Sewing machine
Pins
Thick craft glue (optional)

Babies and toddlers explore their world by the look and feel of things and by the sounds and smells around them. This blanket features bright pastel colors, soft and fuzzy textures, chewy plastic and even a tiny mirror for kids to see themselves.

The theme of this small quilt is the sea world. You can create your own theme through the colors and objects you choose.

My granddaughter, Sandy Hall, took to this little quilt immediately. She pulled it over her head for peekaboo, munched on the teething ring and hugged it securely for nap time. She liked discovering its surprises. So did the toddler shown here, who played with the Blankie during the photo shoot for this book.

The quilt is small, so it can easily be dragged around; flat, so it can be slept upon; and entirely washable, so it can be kept clean. True, it doesn't have sounds or smells. But you can change that by adding a rattle, music box or other safe object.

This tiny quilt can be made with scraps of fleece and various baby toys. Be certain that you firmly sew each object onto the quilt. Use strong thread, and double knot it securely. A child certainly will chew and pull on each part. Here's a rule: If you think your stitching is firmly sewn, repeat it three more times to be sure.

Cut

YOU WILL NEED THE FOLLOWING PATTERN PIECES: Large Bubble, Small Bubble, Fish, Sea Urchin, Mirror Frame, Teething Ring Loop

1. From the pastel green fleece cut an 18" x 18" square for the blanket.

2. From the light blue fleece cut one Mirror Frame and one Small Bubble.

3. From the lime green fleece cut one Mirror Frame and one Sea Urchin.

4. From the gold fleece cut one Fish.

5. From the white fleece cut one Large Bubble.

6. From the cream fleece cut one Teething Ring Loop.

Bind

1. Fit the folded binding strip to one side of the quilt. Leave a ¾" overlap at the start.

2. Hand baste or pin the binding ½" along one side of the quilt, and sew all the way to the quilt edge.

3. Open the binding. Fold it and fit it onto the next quilt side. Make a mitered 45-degree (diagonal) angle at the corner on front and back.

4. Pin and baste in place.

5. Fit the binding all the way around the Blankie, basting (or pinning) as you go. Align the fold to the blanket edge so the front and back edges match on the stitch line.

6. At the corner where the edges meet, open the beginning binding, fold along the edge, and fold again to hide raw edges. Trim the other binding end that went around the quilt to ½". Fold the ½" end inward to hide raw edges. Fold 45-degree folds so the inside corner edges meet. Sew the corner angles to secure.

7. Set the sewing machine to a long zigzag stitch. Using orange thread, sew along the inside binding edge all around the quilt.

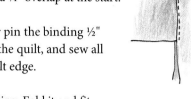

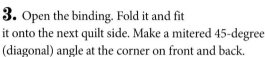

TIP: To make your own binding, cut a strip 5" wide and 72" long (pieced if necessary in two 36" pieces). Fold and press a ½" hem on both lengthwise sides. Fold and press lengthwise down the center of the strip.

Embellish

● MIRROR

1. Match the blue and green Mirror Frame pieces, right sides together.

2. Machine sew around the inside edge with a ¼" seam allowance. This seam keeps the fleece from stretching out so the mirror stays in place.

3. Turn pieces right side out to conceal stitching and match the edges.

4. Place the frame over the mirror and pin in place.

5. Hand stitch or use a zipper foot to machine sew the mirror in place.

TEETHING RING

1. Fold the joining strip lengthwise.

2. Fold it again. Sew the edges together.

3. Loop the strap around the teething ring's opening.

4. Sew the strap ends firmly together.

5. Firmly hand sew the strip in place on the quilt.

TIP: To machine sew the strip, fold it lengthwise and zigzag sew the length. Place it on the quilt and zigzag stitch ½" of it onto the quilt. Loop the strap around the fish, butt-join the ends and hand sew closed.

BUBBLE

1. Place the blue Bubble on top of the white Bubble.

2. Hand or machine applique the blue Bubble in place.

3. Place the white Bubble on the quilt, then hand or machine sew it in place.

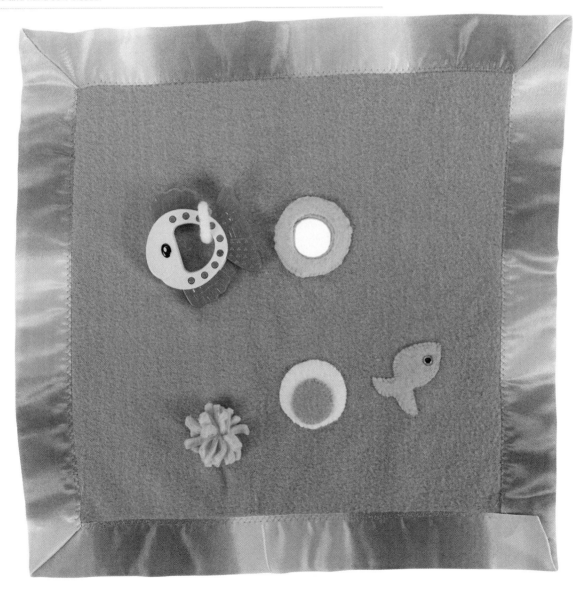

• SEA URCHIN

1. Run a threaded needle through the center of each strip.

2. Pull the thread tightly and wrap it around the gathered joint, then sew and knot the thread.

3. Sew Sea Urchin firmly to the quilt.

• FISH

1. Poke a hole in the fish shape for the eye post.

2. Insert the eye post. Add a dab of craft glue to the washer to secure the eye.

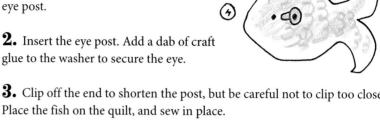

3. Clip off the end to shorten the post, but be careful not to clip too closely. Place the fish on the quilt, and sew in place.

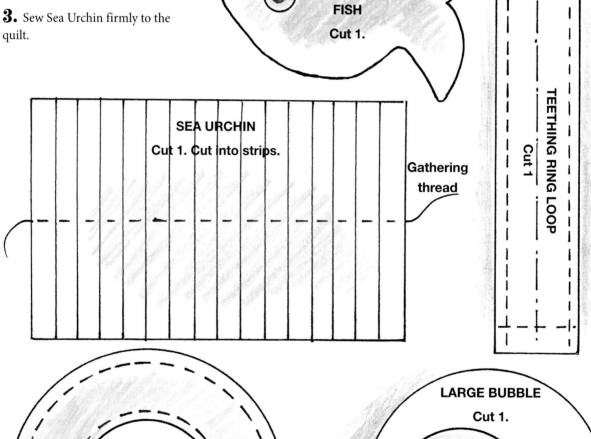

Insert eye.

**FISH
Cut 1.**

**SEA URCHIN
Cut 1. Cut into strips.**

Gathering thread

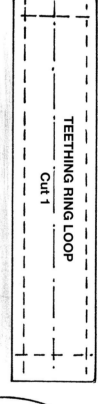

**TEETHING RING LOOP
Cut 1**

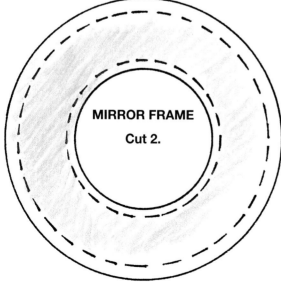

**MIRROR FRAME
Cut 2.**

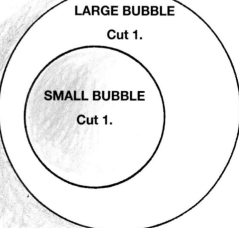

**LARGE BUBBLE
Cut 1.**

**SMALL BUBBLE
Cut 1.**

Stuffed Toy Quilts

The usual task of most quilts is to repose until needed as bedding. These quilts do more: They are interactive. The Circus Train Wall Hanging and the ABC Quilt can stay on the bed or hang on the wall so a child can pop the stuffed toys in and out of the pockets. The circus toys are typical of those a child would see at the circus. The ABC Quilt's stuffed toys teach children their alphabet letters.

CHAPTER

3

Circus Train Wall Hanging

Materials

FABRIC
1½ yd. pre-quilted, double-sided white fabric

½ yd. clear vinyl

½ yd. tear-away stabilizer

½ yd. green metallic fabric

⅓ yd. gold and purple striped poly-cotton fabric

¼ yd. gold felt

9" x 15" scraps of each of the following:
  gold fabric
  orange fabric

9" x 12" piece of each of the following:
  rainbow print fabric
  coral fabric
  green checked print fabric
  light blue felt
  bright pink felt
  purple felt
  variegated brown felt
  dark brown felt

9" x 9" scrap of purple fabric

6" x 9" scrap of each of the following:
  bright golden yellow fabric
  green print fabric

3" x 9" scrap of bright pink fabric

3" x 9" scrap of lime green fabric

BATTING
Football-sized wad of fiberfill

EMBELLISHMENTS
6 yd. gold braid trim, ½" wide

2 yd. red metallic ribbon, ¼" wide

2 yd. of ½" braid

8" x 12" piece of stiff plastic

Scraps of lace

Scraps of felt left over from toys

Scraps of colored braid, rickrack or cord

1 bottle red squeeze paint

5 peach-colored miniature ribbon roses

1 yd. coral ribbon, ½" wide

40 glass jewels, ¼" diameter

9 pairs of hook and loop tape

18 buttons: 6 orange, 6 bright pink, 6 yellow, 1" diameter

1 Chenille stem

NOTIONS
6 yd. doubled-edge blanket binding, 3" wide

Threads in coral and white

Pencil

TOOLS AND SUPPLIES
Ruler	Glue, glue gun
Fabric glue	Scissors
Sewing machine	Needle
Paper hole punch	Tailor's chalk
Dowel	

The circus epitomizes colors, thrills and exotic sights. Years ago, circuses rolled down towns' main streets in colorfully painted wagons pulled by horses or elephants to let everyone know they were in town. Clowns zoomed around on unicycles. Trapeze artists dressed in satins and feathers rode the elephants to town. This image lingers in this simplified quilt design.

When made with the materials shown, this quilt is best suited as a wall hanging because it includes fragile fabrics, trim that might bleed color when wet, glued-on gold braid and vinyl material. For a wash-and-play quilt, substitute a sturdy net for the clear vinyl, bias tape for the gold rope ring and embroidery for the squeeze paint.

The wagons are sewn onto the quilt with open tops for holding circus performers and animal toys, and vinyl sides for visibility. One pattern is used to make all nine Wagons. Choices in fabric color and trim customize each Wagon. The stuffed circus toys can entertain children in or out of their Wagons.

Measure, Mark and Cut

YOU WILL NEED THE FOLLOWING PATTERN PIECES: Wagon, Wagon Top, Wagon Side, Wagon Bottom, Wagon Wheel, Tent, Tent Flag, Bear, Clown, Acrobat, Seal, Camel, Lion, Lion Nose, Pony, Pony Tail, Giraffe, Giraffe Horns, Giraffe Ears, Giraffe Tail, Elephant, Elephant Ear

● FABRIC

1. From the quilted background cut a piece of fabric 42" x 54". Measure and mark a rod pocket 2" from top.

2. From the gold and purple striped fabric cut one Tent. Leave ½" seam allowances.

3. From the orange fabric cut three Wagon Tops, four Wagon Sides, one Wagon Bottom and one Tent Flag.

4. From the bright golden yellow fabric cut two Wagon Sides and one Wagon Bottom.

5. From the coral fabric cut five Wagon Sides and one Wagon Bottom.

6. From the rainbow print fabric cut two Wagon Bottoms and three Wagon Sides.

7. From the purple fabric cut two Wagon Sides, one Tent Flag and two Wagon bottoms.

8. From the green print fabric cut two Wagon Tops.

9. From the lime green print cut one Wagon Bottom.

10. From the metallic gold fabric cut three Wagon Tops, one Wagon bottom and two Wagon Sides.

11. From the bright pink fabric cut one Wagon Top and one Tent Flag.

12. From the metallic green fabric cut 18 circles for Wheel covers, each 3½" in diameter.

13. From the vinyl, cut nine 5½" x 7½" rectangles of vinyl for the wagons.

14. From the tearaway stabilizer, cut nine 5½" x 7½" rectangles for the wagons.

15. On each piece of stabilizer, trace the pattern dashed lines: Top A, Bottom B, Right Side C, Left Side D.

● PLASTIC

1. Cut out 18 stiff plastic circles, 2" in diameter, for the wheels. I used a clear gift box.

2. Use a notebook hole punch to make six adjoining holes that form one large hole in the center of each wheel.

Sew

● CIRCUS TOYS

1. Pin a pattern onto a double layer of its corresponding felt or fabric, layered with the wrong sides of the fabric together. Refer to the materials list to match the toys with the correct colors of felt or fabric.

2. Using tiny stitches, straight stitch on the seam line through both layers of felt or fabric. Leave a 1" opening to stuff.

3. Run a pin tip along the stitch line to help tear off paper patterns.

4. Cut out the toy ⅛ " from the seam line. Use a narrow zigzag stitch over the seam line to prevent fraying.

5. Stuff the toy with fiberfill. Stitch the opening closed.

6. Repeat Steps 1 through 5 for the remaining toys.

7. Finish the toys as directed on the pattern pieces.

● CIRCUS WAGONS

TIP: Each Wagon has two or three different colors of fabric sewn on for the Wagon Sides, Top and Bottom. Before you start to stitch, plan each Wagon's fabric combination, and lay the ready-to-sew pieces on the vinyl to double-check how they look.

1. Align the tear-away stabilizer diagram on top of a vinyl Wagon. Match all edges. Fabrics laid under the vinyl will show through both layers. Although the vinyl is on the bottom now, it will be the middle layer on the sewn wagon.

2. With the vinyl on the bottom and the backing on top, slide a right Wagon Side under the right side of the vinyl. Let the right edge of the fabric overlap the side by ½". Overlap the top and bottom lines.

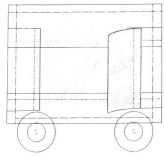

3. Stitch along the Wagon Side pencil line. This will join the right Wagon Side piece.

4. Repeat Steps 2 and 3 for the left Wagon Side piece.

5. Unfold the Wagon Side pieces and finger-press flat.

6. Slide the Wagon Top piece under the vinyl so the top edge overlaps the top seam line by ½" and extends equally on each side of the Wagon.

7. Stitch along the Wagon Top seam line to attach the Wagon Top to the vinyl. The Wagon Top fabric should cover the top edges of the Wagon Sides. Unfold the Top.

8. Slide the Wagon Bottom piece under the vinyl so the lower edge extends below the bottom line ⅜" and extends equally on each side of the Wagon.

9. Stitch the Wagon Bottom along the pencil line to join it to the Wagon. The Wagon Bottom should cover the bottom edges of the Wagon Side pieces so no raw edges show. Unfold the bottom.

10. Finish the edges of the Wagon Top. Fold the fabric over to make a hem, then fold the side hems of the Wagon Top fabric over, then pulling the folded edge over the edge of the Wagon, onto the tear-away stabilizer.

11. Machine topstitch the top hem and the underlying vinyl ⅛" from the edge.

12. Repeat Steps 10 and 11 to complete hems for Wagon Sides and the Wagon Bottom.

13. Repeat Steps 1 through 12 to finish all nine Wagons.

● **WAGON WHEELS**

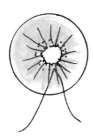

1. Spread glue on the plastic Wheel.

2. For each metallic green fabric circle, hand sew gathering threads around the fabric Wheel shape.

3. Fit the fabric Wheel over the plastic Wheel. Pull the gathering thread tight.

4. Put glue on the back of the Wheel. Sew a knot to secure.

5. Set a weight on the finished Wheel to flatten it.

6. Repeat Steps 1 through 5 to complete the remaining Wheels.

Embellish

Each wagon is decorated differently with braid, ribbon, paint and glued-on rhinestones. Follow the designs pictured or invent your own. Start by tearing away the backing paper from the center window of the Wagon. Remove the side tear-away paper.

For Braid and Ribbon: To attach braid or ribbon, align the braid or ribbon straight across the top of the Wagon with both ends tucked to the backside by ¾". Machine sew across with straight or zigzag stitching to secure. If you arrange the braid or ribbon in loops, in an arc or around the vinyl, first fold the Wagon to find the center. Then pin the braid at this point, or proportion it evenly and pin at high points.

For Glass Jewels: Glue the jewels to the Wagon, and decorate them with the red squeeze paint. Use paint before sewing the Wagons to the quilt in case you smear. (I smeared). Do not put glue or squeeze paint over or near the stitching around the edge, because this seam will be topstitched to join the Wagons to the quilt.

For Circus Toys: Hand sew added pieces such as ears, eyes, tails and costume decorations. In addition to lace, cord and braided trim, I used glass jewels for the Clown's nose and costume buttons, for the Seal's eyes and for the Elephant's saddle.

Join the Wagons

1. Measure the quilt 16" from the bottom edge and 11" from each side.

2. Mark a 20" circle with chalk. Sew or glue the gold braid train track in place.

3. Arrange the Wagons around the track, centered 1½" away from the track and 1" apart. Pin in place.

4. Wrestle the quilt under the sewing machine foot to the top corner of one Wagon. Backstitch over the corner. Sew down one side, across the bottom edge and up the other side, and leave the top open. Backstitch to hold in place.

5. Repeat Step 4 for the remaining Wagons.

6. Arrange the Wheels under the Wagons on the track. Each Wagon's front Wheel is 1" from the next Wagon's rear Wheel.

7. Put buttons in the center of each Wheel. Sew Wheels into place on quilt.

Tent and Tent Flags

1. Position the Tent and Tent Flags on the quilt as shown.

2. Fold a hem under the edges of the Tent. Topstitch around the entire Tent.

3. Fold a hem under each Tent Flag. Topstitch each Tent Flag in place on the quilt.

4. Embellish Tent and Tent Flags as desired. I added gold braid to the Tent, and I used squeeze paint to create posts for the Tent Flags.

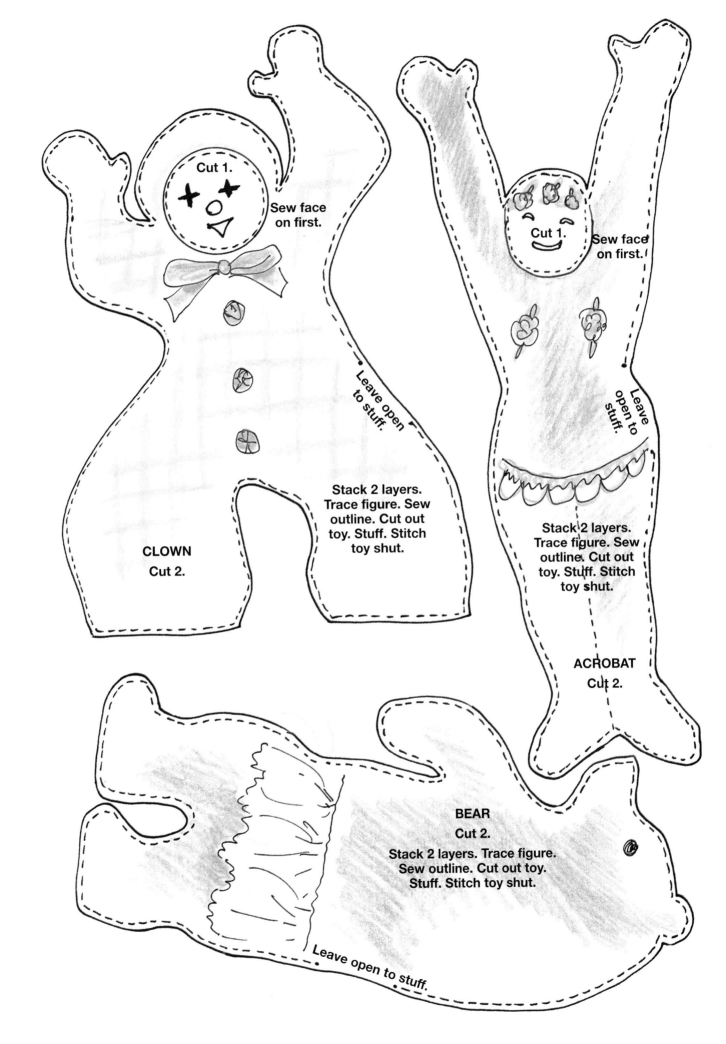

Cut 1.

Sew face
on first.

CLOWN
Cut 2.

Leave open
to stuff.

Stack 2 layers.
Trace figure. Sew
outline. Cut out
toy. Stuff. Stitch
toy shut.

Cut 1.

Sew face
on first.

Leave
open to
stuff.

Stack 2 layers.
Trace figure. Sew
outline. Cut out
toy. Stuff. Stitch
toy shut.

ACROBAT
Cut 2.

BEAR
Cut 2.

Stack 2 layers. Trace figure.
Sew outline. Cut out toy.
Stuff. Stitch toy shut.

Leave open to stuff.

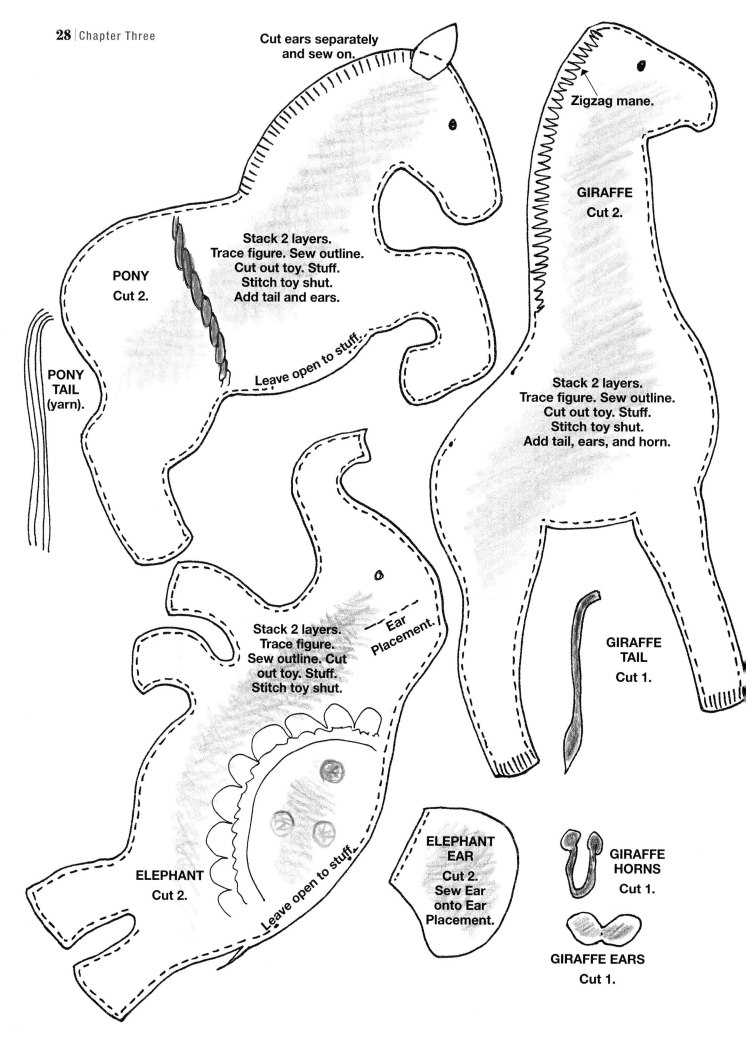

Cut ears separately
and sew on.

Zigzag mane.

PONY
Cut 2.

Stack 2 layers.
Trace figure. Sew outline.
Cut out toy. Stuff.
Stitch toy shut.
Add tail and ears.

GIRAFFE
Cut 2.

PONY
TAIL
(yarn).

Leave open to stuff.

Stack 2 layers.
Trace figure. Sew outline.
Cut out toy. Stuff.
Stitch toy shut.
Add tail, ears, and horn.

Ear
Placement.

Stack 2 layers.
Trace figure.
Sew outline. Cut
out toy. Stuff.
Stitch toy shut.

GIRAFFE
TAIL
Cut 1.

ELEPHANT
Cut 2.

Leave open to stuff.

ELEPHANT
EAR
Cut 2.
Sew Ear
onto Ear
Placement.

GIRAFFE
HORNS
Cut 1.

GIRAFFE EARS
Cut 1.

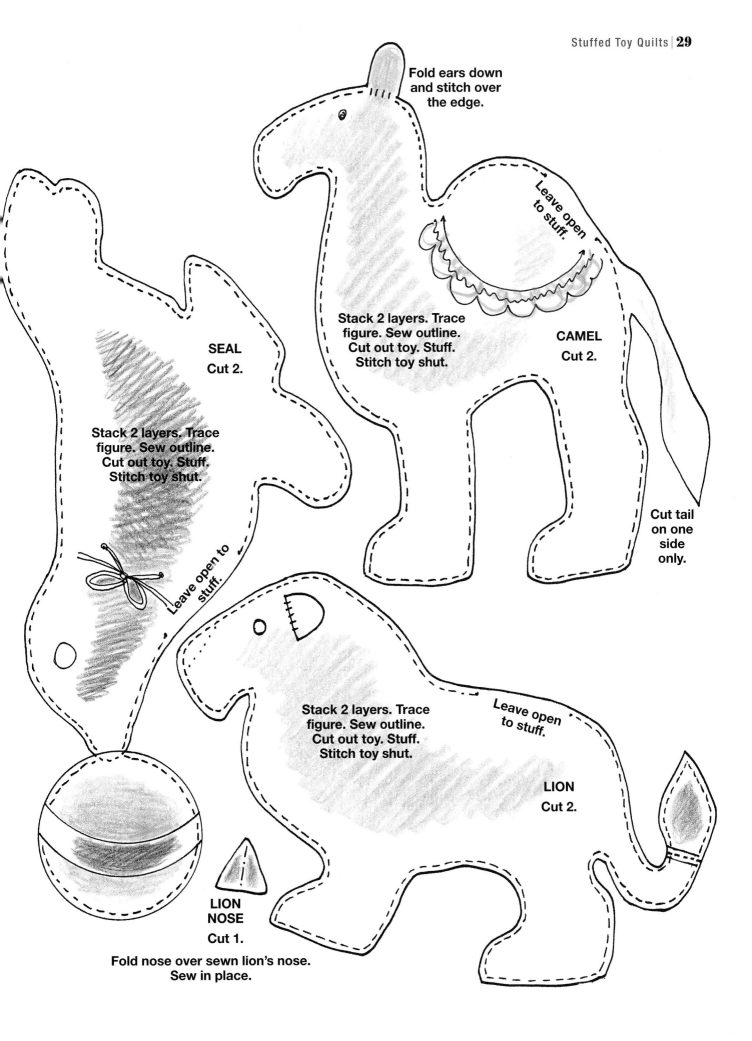

Fold ears down
and stitch over
the edge.

Leave open
to stuff.

Stack 2 layers. Trace
figure. Sew outline.
Cut out toy. Stuff.
Stitch toy shut.

CAMEL
Cut 2.

Cut tail
on one
side
only.

SEAL
Cut 2.

Stack 2 layers. Trace
figure. Sew outline.
Cut out toy. Stuff.
Stitch toy shut.

Leave open to
stuff.

Stack 2 layers. Trace
figure. Sew outline.
Cut out toy. Stuff.
Stitch toy shut.

Leave open
to stuff.

LION
Cut 2.

LION
NOSE

Cut 1.

Fold nose over sewn lion's nose.
Sew in place.

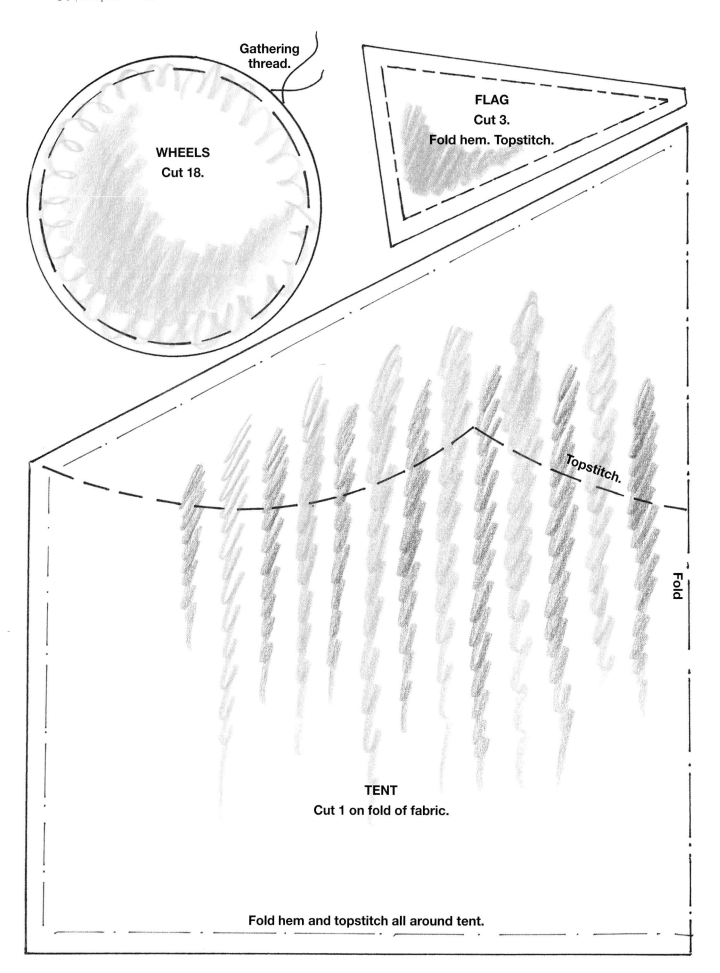

Gathering thread.

WHEELS
Cut 18.

FLAG
Cut 3.
Fold hem. Topstitch.

Topstitch.

Fold

TENT
Cut 1 on fold of fabric.

Fold hem and topstitch all around tent.

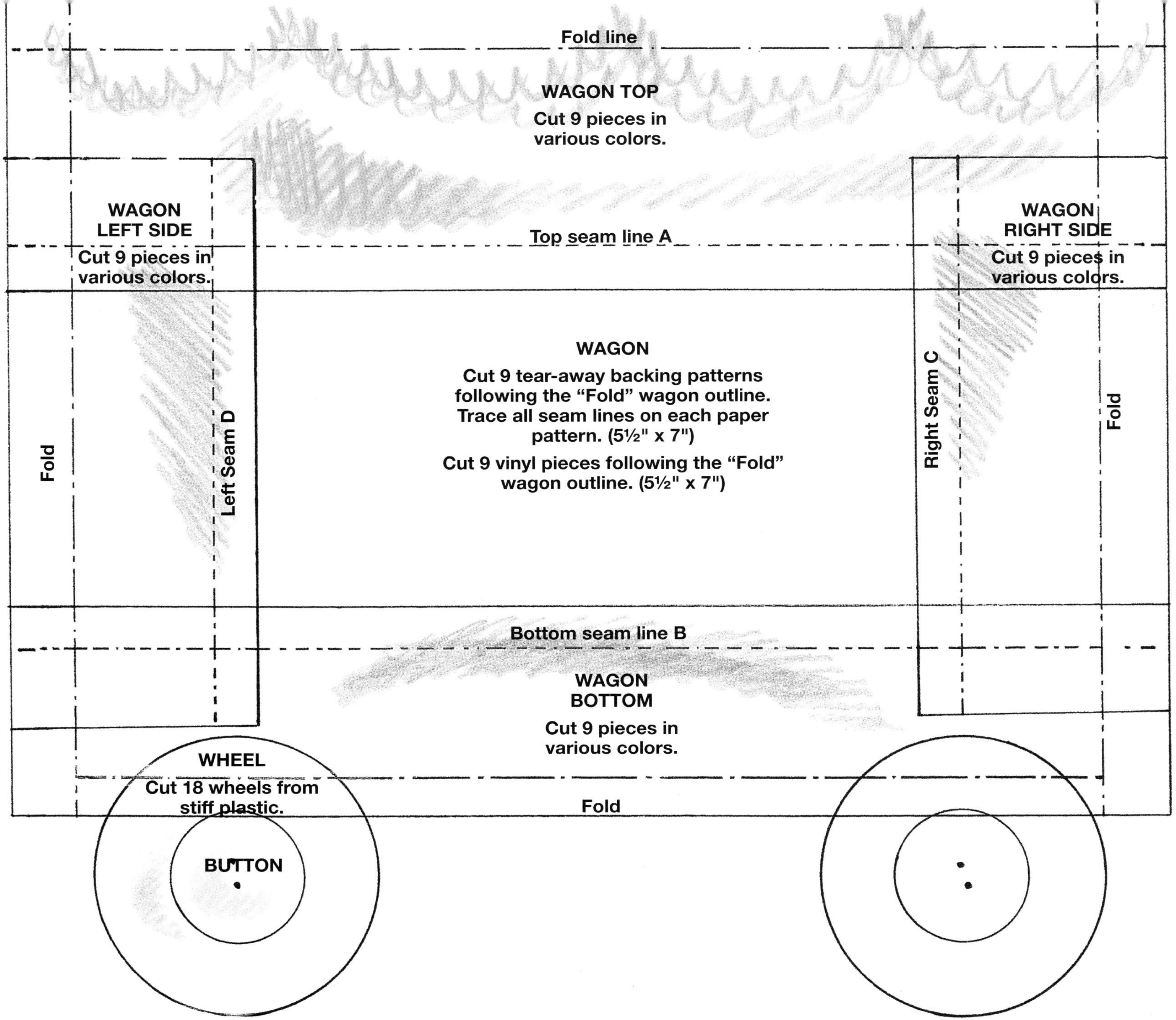

WAGON RIGHT SIDE

Cut 9 pieces in various colors.

Fold

Right Seam C

Fold line

WAGON TOP

Cut 9 pieces in various colors.

Top seam line A

WAGON

Cut 9 tear-away backing patterns following the "Fold" wagon outline. Trace all seam lines on each paper pattern. (5½" x 7")

Cut 9 vinyl pieces following the "Fold" wagon outline. (5½" x 7")

Bottom seam line B

WAGON BOTTOM

Cut 9 pieces in various colors.

Fold

WHEEL

Cut 18 wheels from stiff plastic.

BUTTON

Left Seam D

WAGON LEFT SIDE

Cut 9 pieces in various colors.

Fold

ABC Quilt

Materials

FABRIC

2 yd. (42" wide) red, double-sided quilted fabric

1½ yd. off-white duck cloth

2 yd. dual-sided fusible web

½ yd. of each of the following:
  bright green cotton
  orange cotton
  black cotton

¼ yd. of each of the following:
  light blue cotton
  brown cotton
  tan cotton

12" x 12" scrap of red print

5" x 15" scraps of each of the following:
  bright yellow cotton
  pea green cotton print
  orange/pink/white print
  tan corduroy
  purple
  metallic gold
  brown/gold print
  light yellow cotton
  brown/gray print
  cobalt blue cotton
  brown velveteen
  bright pink
  silver/black holiday polyester
  white napped fabric

5" x 12" scrap of red cotton

4" x 10" scrap of pink cotton

4" x 4" scraps of each of the following prints:
maroon, lavender, gold and green

3" x 9" scrap of dark green pin-dot print

2" x 9" scrap of dark green cotton

2" x 2" scrap of green cotton

FIBERFILL

Small bag of fiberfill

NOTIONS

Threads in red, coral, orange, golden yellow, metallic gold, light green, bright green, pea green, green, dark green, light blue, sky blue, blue, dark blue, navy blue, dark purple, light purple, dark rose, pink, tan, light brown, brown, dark brown, variegated colored thread, variegated gold metallic thread, black, white

27" bright blue jacket zipper with double ends

EMBELLISHMENTS

20 yd. red grosgrain ribbon, ⅝" wide

Black squeeze paint (optional)

Handful of florist's marbles (optional)

TOOLS AND SUPPLIES

Tailor's chalk

Pencil

Yardstick

Pins

Tape measure

Scissors

Sewing machine with zipper foot

Embroidery machine/other lettering method

Iron and ironing board

ABC quilts encourage learning games, and kids can play any number of games with this quilt. They can match stuffed objects with the right letters, place toys in corresponding pockets, find small objects that start with the same letters of the alphabet as the pockets, or even hide objects in the pockets and guess where they are hidden. When the kids are done playing, all of the stuffed toys store safely in the zippered pocket.

The finished size is 38" x 53". Twenty-five canvas pockets and the large, zippered pocket at the bottom mark off the alphabet and hold all of the stuffed objects. The canvas-like duck cloth makes sturdy pockets that don't require stabilizer to embroider. If you choose a lighter-weight fabric, you will need to fuse on backing to stabilize satin stitching and provide greater stability for the pockets.

The pockets are easier to make than they may appear at first glance. They are applied in five long rows, and vertical grosgrain ribbons separate them into 25 individual pockets. A Brother® embroidery machine sewed the letters, but they could be hand or machine embroidered, or even stenciled on.

To simplify construction, use a pre-quilted, double-sided quilted fabric for the background. You can buy single-sided quilted fabric and add a backing, or you can make a traditional-style layered quilt in your own colors and sew on pockets.

Use glossy machine embroidery threads to satin stitch the appliqués. A strong background color requires strong thread colors to outline the appliqués. A darker shade of the object's color often is a good choice. Or choose a satin stitched color that adds detail, such as shown on the Car or the Shoe.

The fabrics shown for the toys and appliqués came from my stash; the materials list reflects those choices. You can select similar colors from your supply, then lay the fabrics together on the quilt so you can balance and harmonize the colors. Or choose fabrics that match the child's personal favorites, such as the color of the Jellybean or scoop of Ice Cream.

Letter-by-letter guide to fabrics and threads

A IS FOR APPLE
Threads: Red (for letters), light green, dark green
Apples: Bright green cotton
Leaves: Dark green cotton

B IS FOR BALL
Threads: Dark blue (letters), light blue, orange
Balls: Light blue cotton
Ball stripes: Orange cotton

C IS FOR CAR
Threads: Black (letters), bright orange
Cars: Bright yellow cotton
Wheels: Black cotton

D IS FOR DUCK
Threads: Medium green (for letters), tan and gold
Duck bodies: Tan cotton
Duck heads: Pin-dot dark green

E IS FOR EGG
Threads: Pink (for letters), orange
Eggs: Orange/pink/white print fabric

F IS FOR FOOTBALL
Threads: Gold and navy (letters), tan
Footballs: Brown cotton

G IS FOR GOLDFISH
Thread: Metallic gold and bright green (letters) orange, black
Goldfish: Orange cotton
Fabric for embroidered letter: 2" x 2" green cotton

H IS FOR HOUSE
Threads: Red (letters), dark brown
House: Pea green cotton print
Doors: Orange cotton
Windows: Light yellow cotton

I IS FOR ICE CREAM
Threads: Tan and coral (for letters) and pink
Ice cream scoops: Pink cotton
Cones: Tan corduroy

J IS FOR JELLYBEAN
Threads: Variegated colors (for letters), dark purple
Jellybeans: Purple

K IS FOR KEY
Thread: Bright orange (for letters), variegated gold metallic
Keys: Metallic gold fabric

L IS FOR LIZARD
Threads: Red (for letters), dark green
Lizards: Brown/gold print

M IS FOR MOON
Threads: Dark blue (for letters), sky blue
Moons: Light yellow cotton

N IS FOR NEST
Threads: Light brown (for letters), blue, multicolor
Nests: Brown/gray print
Eggs: Light blue

O IS FOR ORANGE
Threads: Dark green (for letters), orange
Oranges: Orange cotton
Leaves: Bright green
Note: Use the Ball pattern for the Orange's outline, and the Leaf pattern for the Orange's Leaf.

P IS FOR PEA POD
Threads: Pea green (all)
Pea Pods: Bright green fabric
Note: Use florist's marbles instead of fiberfill stuffing to add a more interesting texture to the Pea Pod.

Q IS FOR QUILT
Threads: Sky blue (for letters), orange
Quilt: Red print, maroon print, lavender print, gold print, green print
Quilt backing: Red print

R IS FOR RAVEN
Threads: Dark rose (for letters), pea green
Ravens: Black cotton

S IS FOR SHOE
Threads: Black (for letters), white, dark blue
Shoes: Cobalt blue cotton

T IS FOR TEDDY BEAR
Threads: Red (for letters), dark brown
Teddy bears: Brown velveteen

U IS FOR UKULELE:
Threads: Light purple (for letters), brown
Ukuleles: Tan cotton

V IS FOR VALENTINE
Threads: Dark rose (all)
Valentine: Bright pink fabric

W IS FOR WAGON
Threads: Green (for letters), black
Wagons: Red cotton
Wheels: Black cotton

X IS FOR X-RAY
Threads: Black (lettering), light purple
X-rays: Silver/black holiday polyester fabric

Y IS FOR YETI
Threads: Sky blue (all)
Yetis: White napped fabric

Z IS FOR ZIPPER
Threads: White (letters), blue
Zipper: Bright blue, 27" jacket zipper with double ends

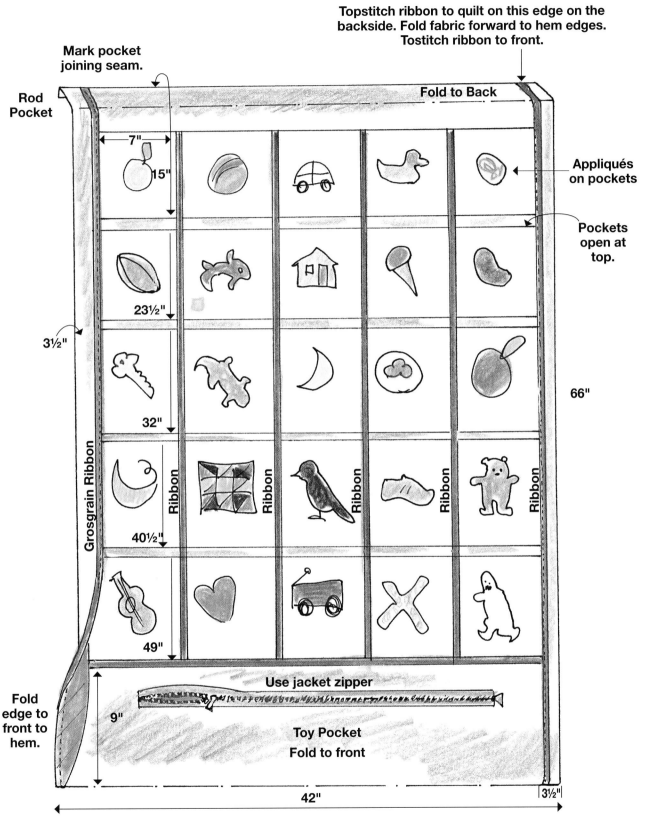

Topstitch ribbon to quilt on this edge on the backside. Fold fabric forward to hem edges. Tostitch ribbon to front.

Mark pocket joining seam.

Rod Pocket

Fold to Back

7"

15"

Appliqués on pockets

Pockets open at top.

23½"

3½"

32"

66"

Grosgrain Ribbon

Ribbon

Ribbon

Ribbon

Ribbon

Ribbon

40½"

49"

Use jacket zipper

Fold edge to front to hem.

9"

Toy Pocket
Fold to front

42"

3½"

ABC Quilt

Cut

YOU WILL NEED THE FOLLOWING PATTERN PIECES: Apple, Leaf, Ball, Ball Stripe, Car, Car and Wagon Wheels, Duck Head, Duck Body, Egg, Football, Goldfish, House, Window, Door, Ice Cream, Cone, Jellybean, Key, Lizard, Moon, Nest, Nest Eggs, Orange, Pea Pod, Pea Pod Stem (embroidery template), Quilt Back, Quilt Triangle, Quilt Center Square, Raven, Shoe, Teddy Bear, Ukulele, Valentine, Wagon, X-Ray, Yeti

● BACKGROUND

1. Cut out the 42" x 66" quilted background piece.

2. Cut out five pocket duck cloth strips that each measure 10" x 40". The added fabric is for the computer sewing machine hoop.

● APPLIQUÉS AND TOYS

Follow the directions on the pattern pieces to cut the fabric for the appliqués and toys. One piece is for each letter's pocket, and the remaining two pieces are used for the toys. Stuffed pieces need added seam allowances, and, in some cases, added allowance for puffing. See patterns for details.

1. From the bright green cotton cut three Apples, three Leaves (for the Orange) and three Pea Pods.

2. From the orange cotton cut three Oranges, three Ball Stripes, three Goldfish and two Doors.

3. From the black cotton cut six Car Wheels, six Wagon Wheels and three Ravens.

4. From the light blue cotton cut three Balls and two Nest Eggs.

5. From the brown cotton cut three Footballs.

6. From the tan cotton cut three Duck bodies and three Ukuleles.

7. From the red print cut one Quilt Back and eight Quilt triangles.

8. From the bright yellow cotton cut three Cars.

9. From the pea green cotton print cut three Houses.

10. From the orange/pink/white print cut three Eggs.

11. From the tan corduroy cut three Cones.

12. From the purple fabric cut three Jellybeans.

13. From the metallic brass fabric cut three Keys.

14. From the brown/gold print cut three Lizards.

15. From the light yellow cotton cut two House Windows and three Moons.

16. From the brown/gray print cut three Nests.

17. From the cobalt blue cotton cut three Shoes.

18. From brown velveteen cut three Teddy Bears.

19. From the bright pink cut three Valentines.

20. From the silver/black holiday polyester cut three X-rays.

21. From the white napped fabric cut three Yetis.

22. From the red cotton cut three Wagons.

23. From the pink cotton cut three Ice Cream scoops.

24. From the maroon print cut eight Quilt Triangles.

25. From the lavender print cut eight Quilt Triangles.

26. From the gold print cut two Quilt Center Squares.

27. From the green print cut eight Quilt Triangles.

28. From the dark green pin-dot print cut three Duck Heads.

29. From the green cotton cut the 2" x 2" square for the embroidered "G" for Goldfish.

30. From the dark green cotton cut three Apple Leaves.

Mark

1. Mark the rod pocket 4" from the top of the quilted background piece.

2. Using tailor's chalk, mark the location of each horizontal strip of pockets on the quilt background. Begin at the top of the quilt, then measure and mark at 15" (A-E); 23½" (F-J); 32" (K-O); 40½" (P-T); and 49" (U-Y). The Zipper pocket folds up to the U-Y line, 9" from the bottom edge.

3. Use tailor's chalk to mark each vertical column for pockets on the quilt background. Starting 9½" from the left edge, draw a vertical mark for the A, F, K, P and U pockets. (The grosgrain ribbon will cover these marks.)

4. Move right 7" and mark another vertical line for the B, G, L, Q and V pockets.

5. Repeat Step 4 for the three remaining columns: C, H, M, R and W; D, I, N, S and X; and E, J, O, T and Y. Like the A, F, K, P and U row, the E, J, O, T and Y row will be 9½" wide.

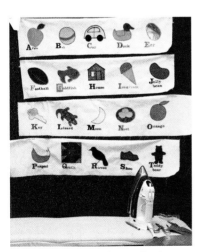

Complete all of the pocket appliqués before attaching the canvas strips to the quilt.

Embroider

1. Align the letters for the words (Apple, Ball, etc.) to be machine embroidered or appliquéd on each pocket. For letter alignment, baste a removable baseline mark 7½" down from the pocket top edge, and be sure to center the mark.

2. Embroider the words. Make each first letter a large capital for emphasis. As you can see, my letter placement is a bit random due to the idiosyncrasies of my sewing machine (and me). The extra fabric allows for fitting the strip into the sewing machine hoop. If you make a mistake, you can replace an individual pocket, because ribbon strips cover the joining between pockets.

3. Repeat Steps 1 and 2 for each pocket.

Try different letter placement, thread colors or even fabric patches to customize embroidered letters.

Appliqué

1. Trace a pocket's image in reverse onto the paper side of fusible web.

2. Iron the fusible web onto the backside of the corresponding fabric.

3. Cut out the image.

4. Tear off the paper backing, then carefully place and iron the image onto the corresponding strip pocket.

5. Choose a contrasting thread as listed to satin stitch the image in place. Add any details.

6. Repeat Steps 1 through 5 for remaining pockets.

TIP: Remember to add details, such as the stripes on the Shoe, the face on the Teddy Bear, and the windows on the Car.

Sew

● DUCK CLOTH POCKETS

1. Fold a ½" hem toward the reverse side of each duck cloth strip. Fold another ½" hem for a total of 1" of fabric. Topstitch.

2. Trim the five appliquéd pocket strips so they measure 7¾" from the top hem to the bottom edge. Draw a ½" seam line along the bottom edge on the backs of the pockets.

3. Lay the top pocket strip face down on the quilt below the quilt top's baseline mark for the pocket.

4. Align the marked pocket seam line with the marked baseline.

5. Sew across and flip up the pocket to hide the seam.

6. Repeat Steps 1 through 5 for each row of pockets.

TIP: You may have to roll the quilt to get it all under the sewing machine foot.

● ZIPPER POCKET

1. Fold the Zipper pocket up from the bottom of the quilt background.

2. Pin the Zipper pocket in place below the fifth pocket row.

3. Cut a 27" slash centered 2" from the top edge of the Zipper pocket front.

4. Unfold the Zipper pocket.

5. On each side of the slash, fold a ¼" hem upward onto the quilt face. This will make finished edges on the back of the Zipper.

6. Position the Zipper over the hemmed slash on the quilt face; pin or tape the Zipper aligned with the hemmed edges.

7. Topstitch the Zipper in place, close to the teeth and along the outside Zipper edges.

8. Topstitch the exposed Zipper ends onto the pocket front.

● RIBBONS

1. Starting at the left edge of the quilt, position the first pocket-separating ribbon vertically over the five pocket strips. Cover the division marks.

2. Tuck the ribbon's top end into the top pocket.

3. Topstitch both edges of the ribbon in place.

4. Repeat Steps 1 through 3 for the remaining vertical ribbons.

5. Place a red ribbon across the unfinished bottom edge of the quilt on the backside, above the Zipper, overlapping by ¼".

6. Stitch the ribbon in place on the bottom edge of the quilt. When the Zipper pocket is flipped up, this will cover the raw edge.

7. Flip the Zipper pocket up. Topstitch the ribbon to the quilt, below the final set of duck cloth pockets. Be sure to cover the vertical ribbon ends.

8. On the reverse side of the quilt, topstitch ribbon over the left edge of the quilt background.

9. Repeat Step 6 for the right edge of the quilt background.

10. Fold one ribbon-finished vertical edge 2" toward the front of the quilt to cover the edges of the pocket strips.

11. Trim away excess fabric that will make the Zipper pocket bulky at each end.

12. Pin the side in place.

13. Topstitch the edge.

14. Repeat Steps 10 through 13 for the other side of the quilt.

● ROD POCKET

1. Fold a 1" hem at the top of the quilt.

2. Fold down another 3" to form a rod pocket.

3. Topstitch the rod pocket to the quilt back.

● STUFFED TOYS

1. Match a completed stuffed toy's front piece with its corresponding back piece. Assemble, applique or embroider added details on toy fronts before joining.

2. Place the front and back pieces together.

3. Follow a ¼" seam allowance and sew around the perimeter of the toy shape. Leave a 1½" opening to turn and stuff the toy.

4. Clip seam allowances on inside corners of the toy to avoid pulling.

5. Carefully turn the toy.

6. Lightly stuff the toy. For the Pea Pod, I used florist's marbles to add interest and texture.

7. Hand sew the 1½" opening shut.

8. Repeat Steps 1 through 7 for each piece of the toy.

9. Sew completed secondary pieces, if applicable, (i.e. the leaf for the apple) onto to the matching toy.

10. Repeat Step 9 for each toy as needed.

TIP: To avoid the hassle of turning, stuffing and finishing toys with small details or tight turns — such as the Apple, Car, Lizard, Moon, Shoe and Ukulele — sandwich all three layers of the toy together as they are to appear on the finished product — face fabric, filler and backing fabric — then sew around the shape, finishing the edges with a satin stitch. Otherwise, you can follow the traditional stitch, turn, stuff and finish method.

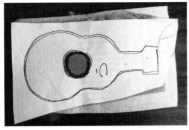

Layer the face fabric, filler and backing fabric. Place the pattern on top. Stitch on the pattern lines.

Remove the pattern piece.

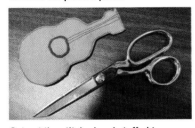

Cut out the stitched and stuffed toy.

Finish the toy by satin stitching the edges.

Embellish

1. Use squeeze paint to add texture and dimension to your toys. I used it to delineate the Window and Door on the House; add eyes to the Goldfish, Lizard and Raven; create faces for the Teddy Bear and Yeti; and add the laces and seam to the Football.

2. Insert finished toys in their corresponding canvas pockets.

TIP: For secure storage, store stuffed toys in the large Zipper pocket.

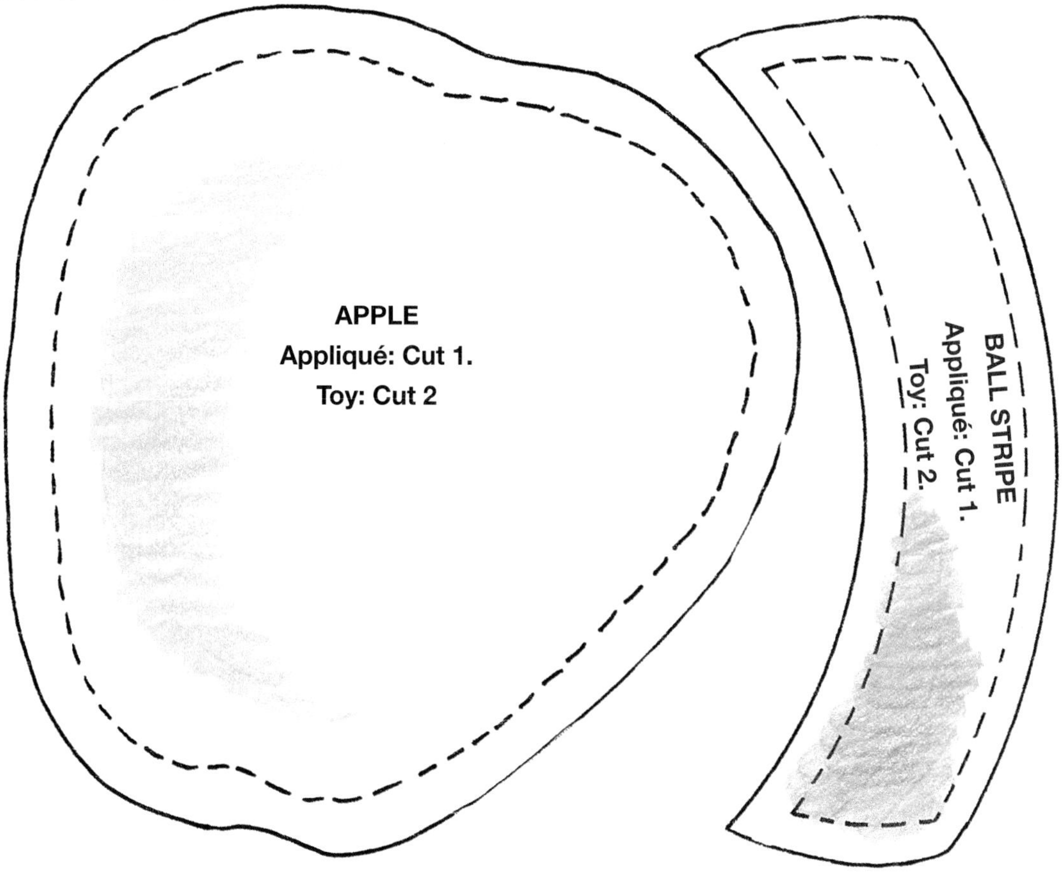

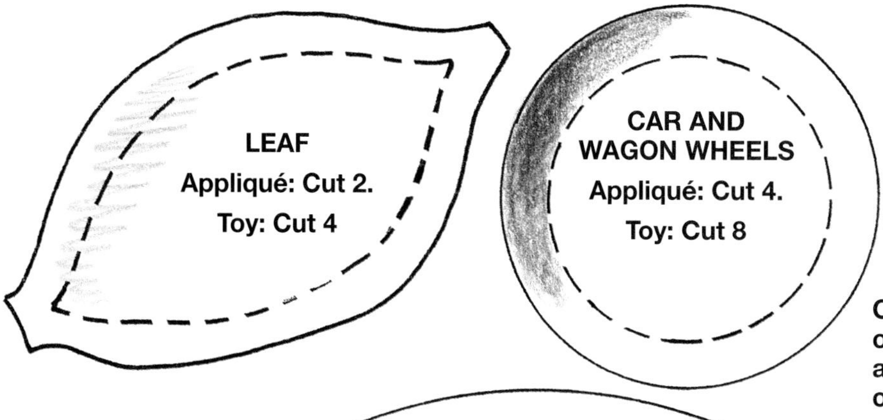

APPLE
Appliqué: Cut 1.
Toy: Cut 2

BALL STRIPE
Appliqué: Cut 1.
Toy: Cut 2.

LEAF
Appliqué: Cut 2.
Toy: Cut 4

**CAR AND
WAGON WHEELS**
Appliqué: Cut 4.
Toy: Cut 8

Cut toy pieces on solid
outlines. Sew ¼" seam
allowances and leave an
opening to turn to stuff.

Cut appliqué pieces on
dashed lines.

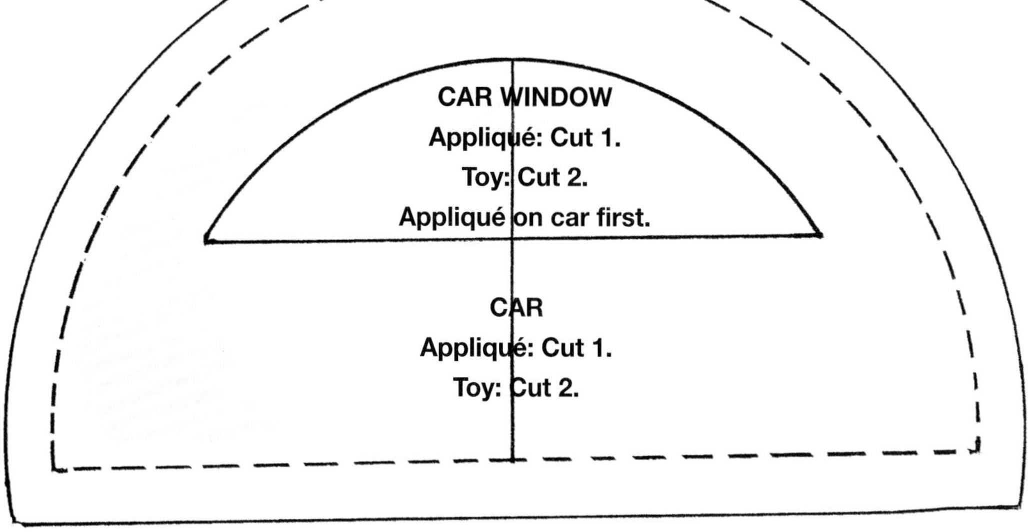

CAR WINDOW
Appliqué: Cut 1.
Toy: Cut 2.
Appliqué on car first.

CAR
Appliqué: Cut 1.
Toy: Cut 2.

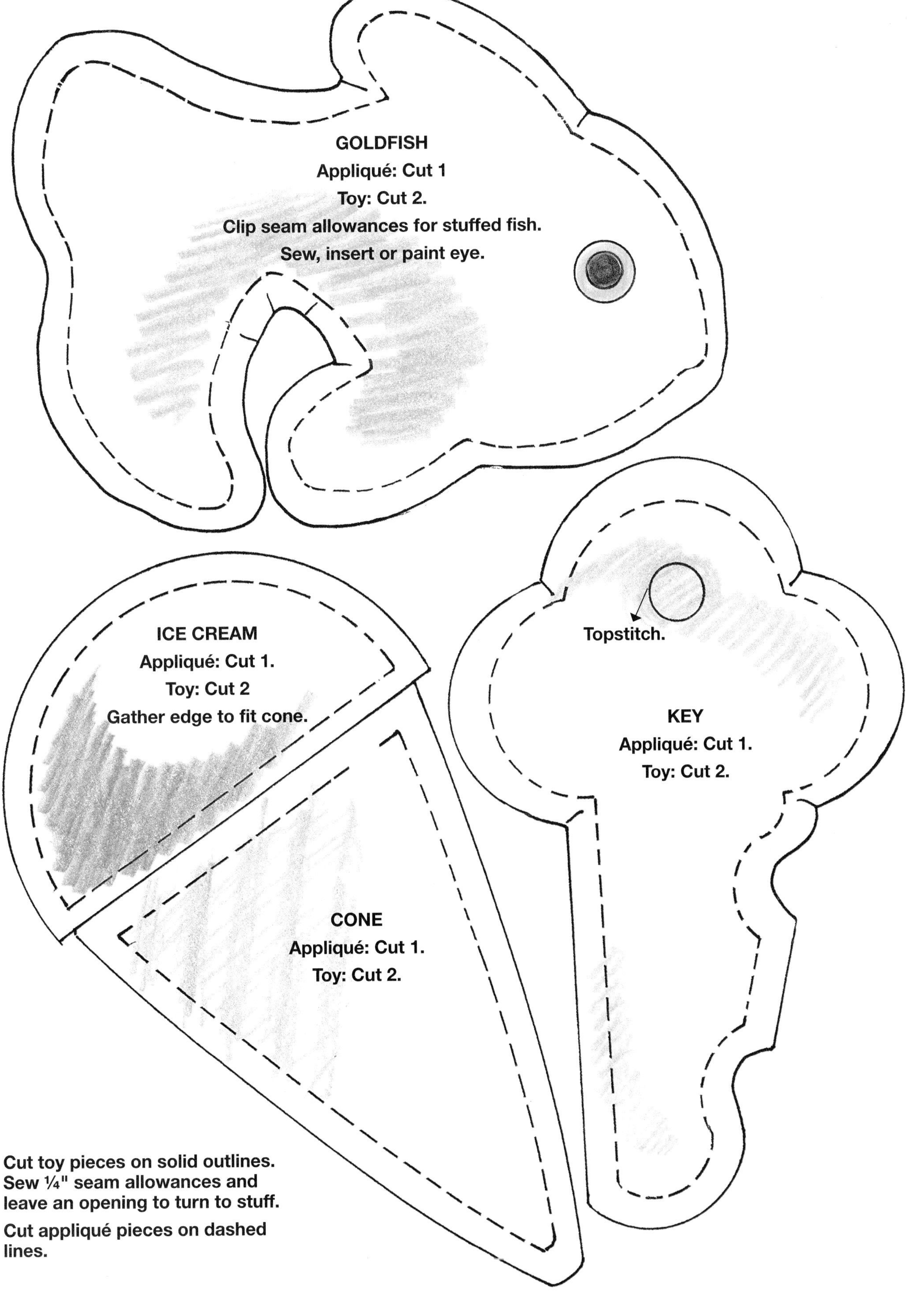

GOLDFISH

Appliqué: Cut 1

Toy: Cut 2.

Clip seam allowances for stuffed fish.

Sew, insert or paint eye.

ICE CREAM

Appliqué: Cut 1.

Toy: Cut 2

Gather edge to fit cone.

Topstitch.

KEY

Appliqué: Cut 1.

Toy: Cut 2.

CONE

Appliqué: Cut 1.

Toy: Cut 2.

Cut toy pieces on solid outlines.
Sew ¼" seam allowances and
leave an opening to turn to stuff.

Cut appliqué pieces on dashed
lines.

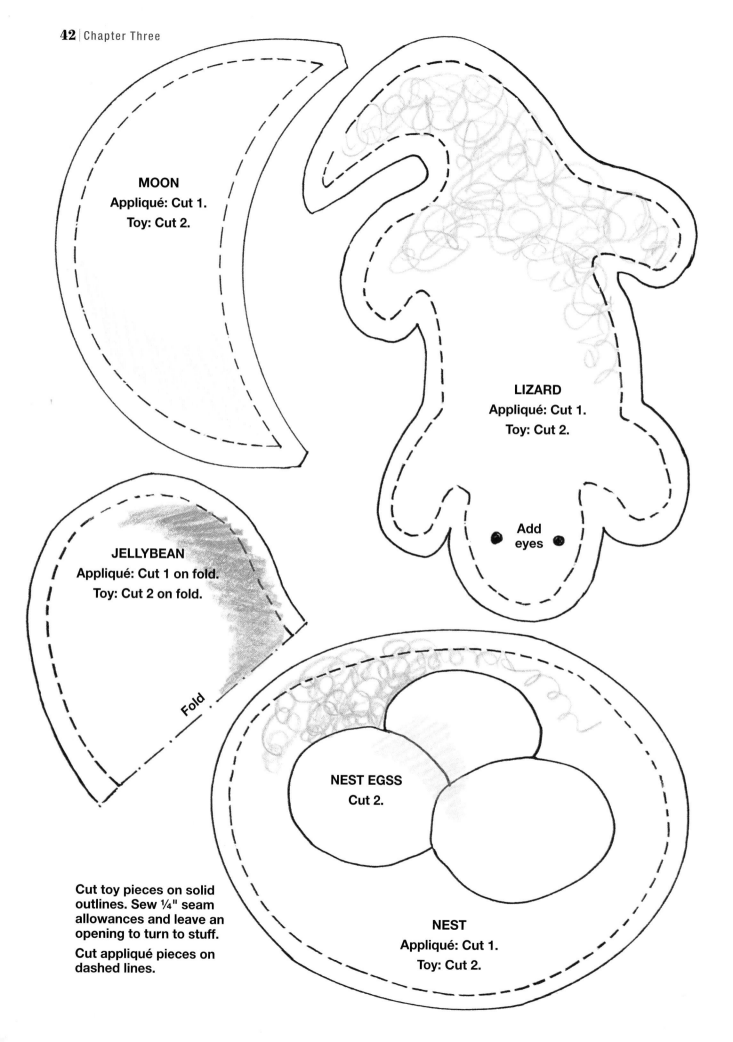

MOON
Appliqué: Cut 1.
Toy: Cut 2.

LIZARD
Appliqué: Cut 1.
Toy: Cut 2.

Add
eyes

JELLYBEAN
Appliqué: Cut 1 on fold.
Toy: Cut 2 on fold.

Fold

NEST EGSS
Cut 2.

NEST
Appliqué: Cut 1.
Toy: Cut 2.

Cut toy pieces on solid
outlines. Sew ¼" seam
allowances and leave an
opening to turn to stuff.

Cut appliqué pieces on
dashed lines.

Cut toy pieces
on solid outlines.
Sew ¼" seam
allowances and
leave an opening
to turn to stuff.

Cut appliqué
pieces on
dashed lines.

DUCK HEAD
Appliqué: Cut 1.
Toy: Cut 2.
Sew eye.

Embroider wing.

DUCK BODY
Appliqué: Cut 1.
Toy: Cut 2.

Fold

FOOTBALL
Appliqué: Cut 1
on fold.

Toy: Cut 2 on fold.

STUFFED QUILT BACK   Cut 1 whole piece.

Diagram to assemble quilt.

CENTER SQUARE
Cut 2.

QUILT TRIANGLES
Cut 16 to
here.

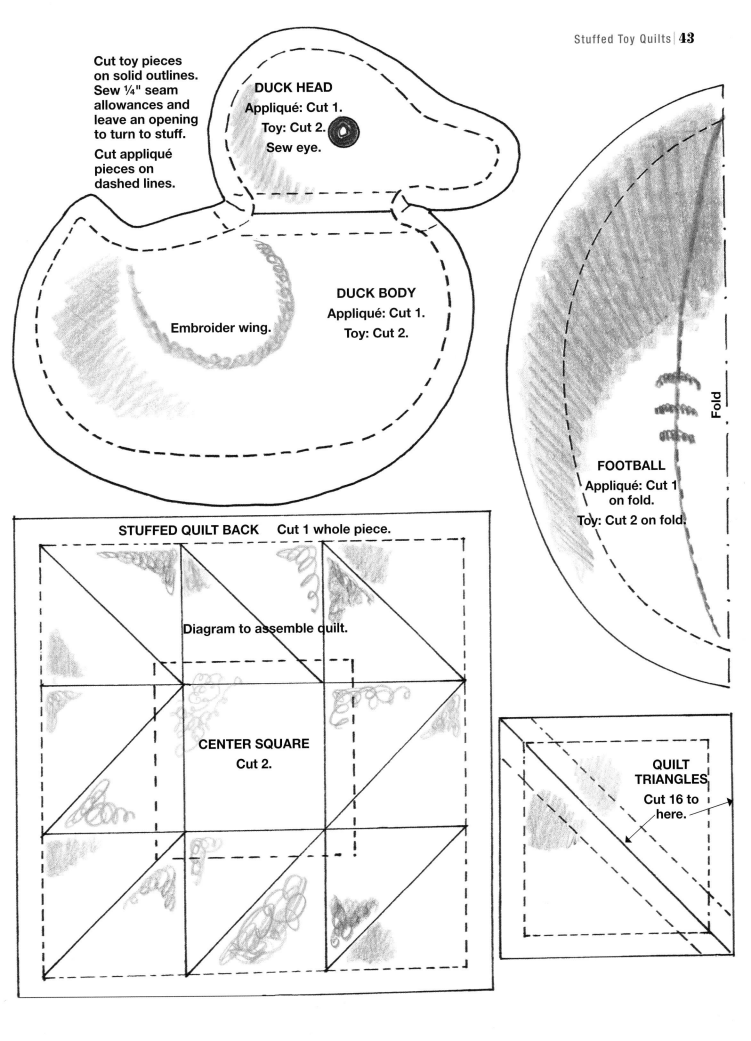

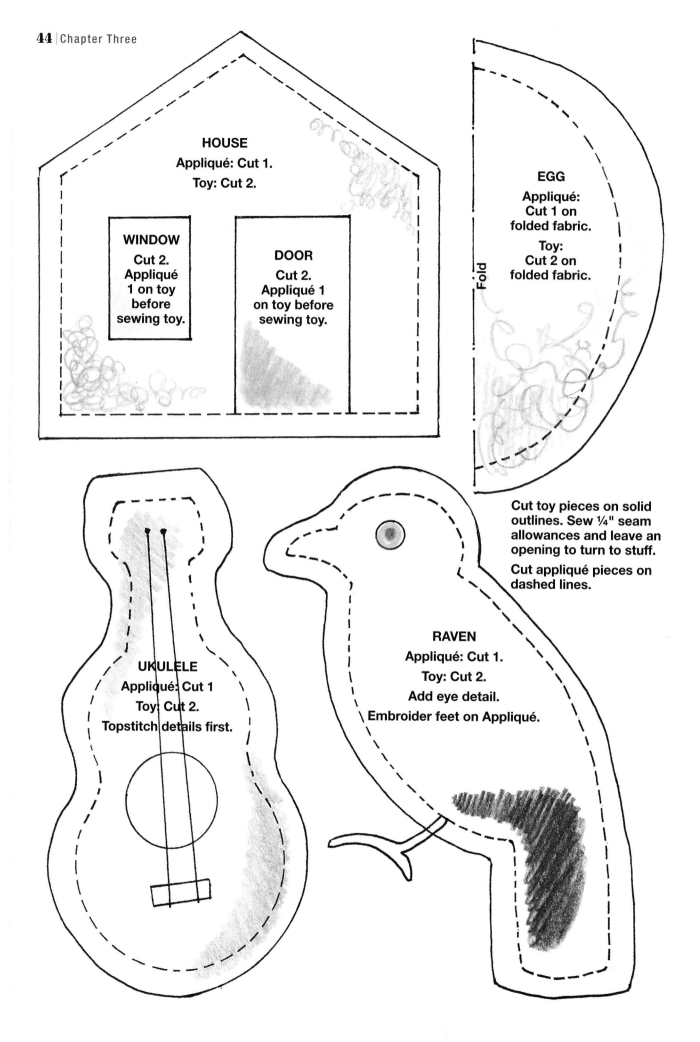

HOUSE
Appliqué: Cut 1.
Toy: Cut 2.

WINDOW
Cut 2.
Appliqué 1 on toy before sewing toy.

DOOR
Cut 2.
Appliqué 1 on toy before sewing toy.

EGG
Appliqué:
Cut 1 on folded fabric.
Toy:
Cut 2 on folded fabric.

Fold

Cut toy pieces on solid outlines. Sew ¼" seam allowances and leave an opening to turn to stuff.

Cut appliqué pieces on dashed lines.

UKULELE
Appliqué: Cut 1
Toy: Cut 2.
Topstitch details first.

RAVEN
Appliqué: Cut 1.
Toy: Cut 2.
Add eye detail.
Embroider feet on Appliqué.

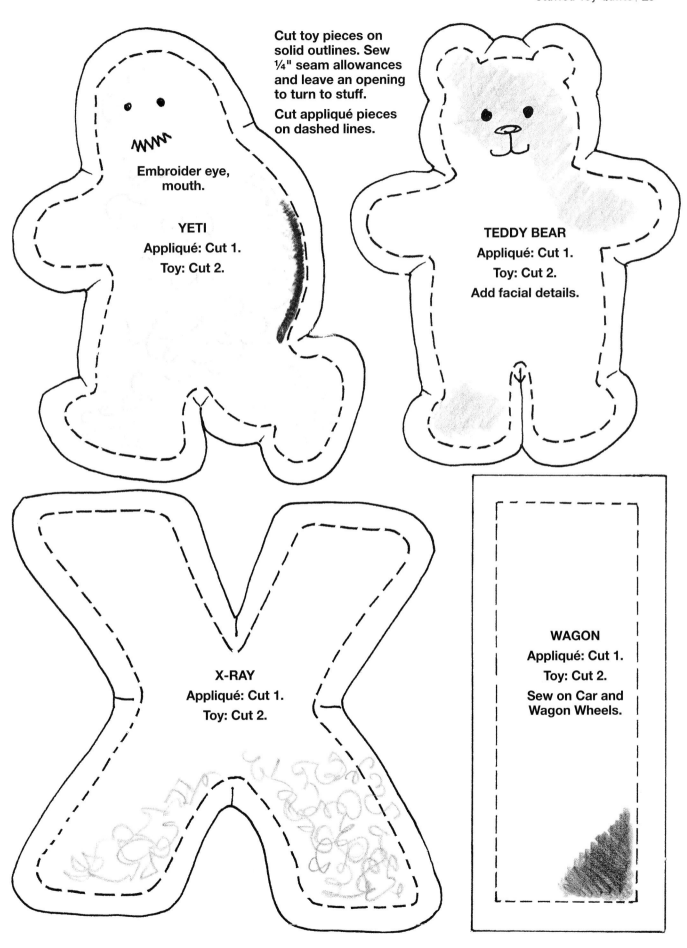

Cut toy pieces on solid outlines. Sew ¼" seam allowances and leave an opening to turn to stuff.

Cut appliqué pieces on dashed lines.

Embroider eye, mouth.

YETI
Appliqué: Cut 1.
Toy: Cut 2.

TEDDY BEAR
Appliqué: Cut 1.
Toy: Cut 2.
Add facial details.

X-RAY
Appliqué: Cut 1.
Toy: Cut 2.

WAGON
Appliqué: Cut 1.
Toy: Cut 2.
Sew on Car and Wagon Wheels.

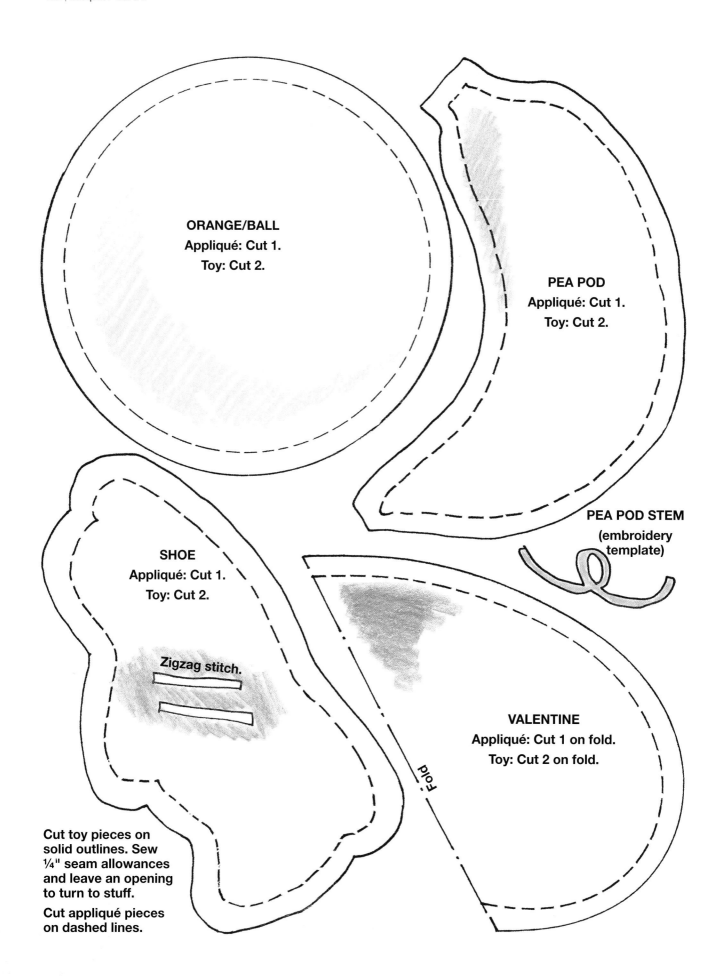

ORANGE/BALL
Appliqué: Cut 1.
Toy: Cut 2.

PEA POD
Appliqué: Cut 1.
Toy: Cut 2.

PEA POD STEM
(embroidery template)

SHOE
Appliqué: Cut 1.
Toy: Cut 2.

Zigzag stitch.

Fold

VALENTINE
Appliqué: Cut 1 on fold.
Toy: Cut 2 on fold.

Cut toy pieces on solid outlines. Sew ¼" seam allowances and leave an opening to turn to stuff.

Cut appliqué pieces on dashed lines.

Make It Mine

Another way to make interactive quilts is to get ideas from the child. You get the pleasure of sewing a quilt for a special child. The child gets to guide the design by choosing images from various projects in the book or borrowing images from elsewhere to appliqué on a personal choice quilt. You can customize the quilt even more by sewing the child's name in the center quilt block.

To give kids even more involvement, let them make their own images that you sew into a personal quilt, pillow fronts, cloth books or whatever comes to mind.

Personal Patchwork Quilt

Materials

FABRIC

1¼ yd. of ABC, 123 block print poly-cotton, 42" wide

½ yd. orange poly-cotton

½ yd. yellow print

¼ yd. lime green poly-cotton

¼ yd. hot pink poly-cotton

¼ yd. peach fabric

¼ yd. off-white fabric

¼ yd. moss green print

¼ yd. rainbow stripe print

¼ yd. purple print

10" x 10" scrap of blue cloud print

10" x 10" scrap of coral fabric

9" x 10" scrap of blue/mauve plaid

6" x 9" scrap of purple/orange stripe

6" x 9" scrap of blue print fabric

6" x 9" scrap of rust print fabric

6" x 9" scrap of white fabric

6" x 8" scrap of red print fabric

6" x 6" scrap of brown fabric

6" x 6" scrap of soft green spotted print

5" x 6" scrap of gold print

4" x 4" scrap of pink flower print

3" x 6" brown print

1" x 2" scrap of orange fabric

STUFFING AND BATTING

1¼ yd. iron-on, lightweight polyester quilt batting, 42" wide

EMBELLISHMENTS AND NOTIONS

Fusible web

Stabilizer for 13 quilt blocks, 8½" x 8½", or 26 sheets of paper

Threads: Pink, light orange, dark purple, fuschia, black, medium blue, brown, bright golden yellow, bright green

Dark brown squeeze paint (optional)

Iron-on letters to spell out recipient's name (optional)

TOOLS AND SUPPLIES

Poster board for templates

Iron and ironing board

Quilt pins

Hand sewing needles

Matching threads

No. 2 pencil

Sharp scissors

Sewing machine

Yardstick

Choose favorite images from this book to make a personal-themed Patchwork Quilt for a child. Select images that relate to the child's interests. The animals on the quilt shown come from three different projects in this book. If the patterns in this book aren't enough choices for you, look through favorite children's books for other images to make your own.

It helps to simplify the pieces to a single color. Select solid images with few skinny parts, as skinny fabric pieces can shift, and they don't show up well. Using fusible web will anchor each appliqué piece in place.

To finish, add the child's name to the name square. Iron-on letters, available in craft stores, are another option. You also can appliqué your own letters or sew quilting letters.

The fun of this quilt is that you can design it yourself. If you vary the colors, be sure to lay them all out together to see if they sing (and zing) well together.

Cut

YOU WILL NEED THE FOLLOWING PATTERN PIECES: Personal Quilt Templates A-E, Frog, Dog, Cat, Rabbit, Elephant, Bear, Raven, Lizard, Goldfish, Duck, Bee, Flower, Butterfly

● TEMPLATES

1. Trace Personal Quilt Templates A, B, C, D and E onto poster board.

2. Cut out each template.

3. Copy and cut out the pattern pieces planned for the quilt. I used the Frog, Dog, Cat, Rabbit, Elephant and Bear patterns designed for this quilt. I also used the Raven (which I turned into a Robin by cutting a small patch of coral fabric by freehand to fit its breast), Lizard, Goldfish and Duck patterns from the ABC Quilt, and the Bee, Flower and Butterfly patterns from the Flower Quilt project.

● FUSIBLE WEB

1. Trace the appliqué images onto the fusible web in reverse. Use a light box or day-lit window to trace the images onto the fusible web.

2. Cut out each image, leaving a 1" margin around each image.

● FABRIC

1. From the ABC, 123 block print fabric cut a 42" x 42" square for the quilt backing.

2. From the orange fabric cut or tear the following sashing strips: two 1¾" x 45" (or piece this strip at a corner); two 1¾" x 30", and 20 1¾" x 9".

3. From the lime green fabric cut or tear 4" wide strips for the border. Cut those border strips into eight pieces that are 4" x 12" and eight pieces that are 4" x 6".

4. From the hot pink fabric cut 16 border strip pieces that are 3" x 4".

5. From the yellow print fabric cut one Cat, one pair of Bee wings and two 8½" x 8½"squares. Cut the squares in half diagonally.

6. From the coral fabric cut one piece of fabric to fit as the Robin's breast and one 8½" x 8½" square. Cut the square in half diagonally.

7. From the blue cloud print cut one 8½" x 8½" square. Cut that square in half diagonally.

8. From the peach fabric cut two 8½" x 8½" squares.

9. From the off-white fabric cut two 8½" x 8½" squares

10. From the moss green print cut four 8½" x 8½" squares.

11. From the blue/mauve plaid print cut one 8½" x 8½" square.

12. From the purple print cut four 6¼" x 6¼" right triangles and one Elephant.

13. From the red print cut two Butterflies.

14. From the pink flower print cut one Flower.

15. From the soft green spotted print cut one Frog.

16. From the purple and orange striped fabric cut one Lizard and one Bee body.

17. From the blue print cut one Rabbit.

18. From the white fabric cut one Duck body.

19. From the orange fabric cut one Duck's bill.

20. From the rust print cut one Dog.

21. From the brown fabric cut one Bear.

22. From the brown print cut one Robin's body.

Customize this quilt with fabrics, colors and appliqués to suit the recipient's tastes.

Appliques add interest to the quilt. You can add details, such as facial features.

Trace

1. Use a pencil to trace Template A in the center of the reverse side of the peach, off-white, moss green print and blue/mauve plaid squares. The outline will serve as the seam allowance mark.

2. Use a pencil to trace Template B on the reverse side of the coral, yellow print and blue cloud print right triangles. The outline will serve as the seam allowance mark.

3. Use a pencil to trace Template C on the reverse side of the purple print right triangles. The outline will serve as the seam allowance mark.

4. Use the yardstick to mark lengthwise seam lines 1¼" apart on the back of the long orange sashing strips.

5. Trace Template D on the back of the 20 short orange sashing strips.

6. Use the yardstick to mark ½" seam lines along one lengthwise edge of the lime green border strips. Border strip lengths aren't marked because you may need to jury rig them to fit when applied.

7. Use Template E to trace seam lines on the back of the hot pink border strip pieces.

Appliqué

1. Place a fusible web image on the back of the matching appliqué fabric.

2. Iron the web in place.

3. Cut out the fused image.

4. Tear off the backing paper.

5. Place the backed image on a quilt block. Iron it in place.

6. Repeat Steps 1 through 5 for each appliquéd word or image.

7. Align stabilizer (or two pieces of paper) on the back of a block.

8. Select a coordinating thread to outline the image.

9. Use a sewing machine to satin stitch around the image and appliqué it in place.

Embellish

1. Sew eyes on animals, using the same color thread to satin stitch around the appliqué. Or you can paint the eyes and facial features onto the figures using brown acrylic paint.

2. To add a name to the quilt, use iron-on letters, or appliqué and sew the name in the center block.

Sew

Arrange the blocks in rows for easy assembly.

● BLOCKS

TIP: The blocks and sashing are assembled in diagonal rows, starting with the longest row, which contains the Bear, Dog, Name, Elephant and Frog blocks.

1. Match the Bear block's lower left edge with a short sash strip, placing right sides together.

2. Match the drawn seam lines on the reverse sides of the fabric.

3. Pin at the marked corners and across the seam line.

4. Sew the sash strip to the block.

5. Repeat Steps 1 through 4 for the Dog, Name, Elephant and Frog blocks.

6. Sew another sash strip to the upper right Frog block.

7. Sew a purple triangle to the Bear block sash.

8. Join the Bear block to the Dog block sash.

9. Join the Dog block to the Name block sash.

10. Join the Name block to the Elephant block sash.

11. Join the Elephant block to the lower Frog block sash.

12. Join the purple triangle to the upper Frog sash to complete the row.

13. Revisit Steps 1 through 12 to assemble the remaining rows as follows:
- Row 2: yellow triangle, sash, Duck block, sash, Rabbit block, sash, Bee block, sash, blue cloud triangle.
- Row 4: coral triangle, sash, Lizard block, sash, Cat block, sash, Fish block, sash, yellow triangle.
- Row 1: yellow triangle, sash, Flower block, sash, blue cloud triangle.
- Row 5: coral triangle, sash, Robin block, sash, yellow triangle.

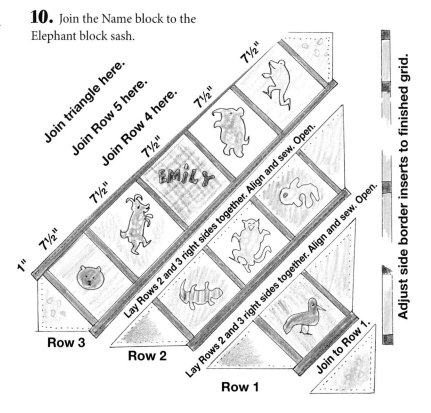

QUILT TOP

1. Align a long sashing strip to each side of Row 3.

2. Match seam markings for each strip and block.

3. Sew the strip to the block. For accurately aligned cross sashes, use a pencil to mark short sash seams on the back of each long sash strip.

4. Align Row 2 blocks to the left-side sash on Row 3.

5. Match the marks with the Row 2 sashing seams.

6. Pin and sew the Row 2 blocks to the left-side sash on Row 3.

7. Repeat Steps 4 through 6 to attach Row 4 to the right-side sash on Row 3.

8. Join a medium long sashing strip to Rows 2 and 4. Mark the seams.

9. Align Row 1 to Row 2, including marks and seams. Sew the rows.

10. Align Row 4 to Row 5, including marks and seams. Sew the rows.

11. Align a short sash strip to the top left of the Butterfly block, then sew it to the block.

12. Align a small purple triangle to the sashing strip on the Butterfly block. Sew it in place.

13. Repeat Steps 11 and 12 for Row 5.

Layer

1. Place the quilt backing face down. Smooth it out.

2. Spread the batting on the wrong side of the backing.

3. Smooth out the batting. Trim it to size.

4. Lay the assembled quilt top face up on the filler. Smooth it into place.

5. Iron the fusible batting in place. If you are using nonfusible batting, pin the layers together with quilting or safety pins.

6. Hand or machine stitch in the ditch (hidden on the seam line) along all the sashing edges to secure the layers. Remove pins as you sew. The quilt pictured was hand quilted for a pebbly effect. Machine quilting probably is sturdier.

Trim

1. Use the yardstick to trim straight edges on the quilt.

2. Draw a straight line along the triangle edges and across the center of the sashing joinings along the outside raw edges. Including the binding, the finished quilt will measure about 40".

3. Trim a straight line.

Bind

If you are incredibly accurate in measuring and sewing, you can assemble the binding strip by measurement. If you sew like I do, carefully but casually, try these steps:

1. Iron ½" hems on each side of the hot pink binding pieces to measure 1½" x 4".

2. Match the binding pieces to the sashing joinings, right sides together. Save four binding pieces for corners.

3. Lay the lime green border strips between the hot pink pieces.

4. Pin the lime green strips to the hot pink pieces where they meet.

5. Sew strips and pieces together.

6. Sew a hot pink piece at each end of two rows.

7. Pin the shorter assembled binding row to the top of the quilt. Align with the sashing joinings. Sew.

8. Repeat for the bottom edge.

9. Flip open the binding, and pin it in place.

10. Match the longer binding, with hot pink rectangles at each end, to the quilt edges.

11. Align the hot pink squares to the sashing joints. This strip will be about 1" shorter than the unfolded binding's top and bottom.

12. Use Template E to measure the 1½" width of the binding.

13. Match Template E to the binding seam. Fold the binding over it.

14. Hand fold a ½" hem on the binding's back edge. Pin it in place. This should align with the binding seam on the front.

15. Keep sliding the template along to fold the binding over it. Do so all around the quilt.

16. Fold the top and bottom bindings over first. Fold the sides next so that the hot pink pieces fold over the bindings at the corners.

17. To machine sew, fold the binding face to face and sew across, staying even with the folded top binding. Do the same for bottom corners. To hand sew, fold the pink pieces at the corners over the edge, tuck in the raw edges to align with the top or bottom binding and blind stitch.

18. Tuck a hem in the binding on the back of the quilt so the binding edge just barely covers the seam line. Hand stitch in place, or machine stitch in the ditch on the front.

Finish

1. Hand or machine quilt the bindings at seam lines and on the bindings where stitching occurs.

2. Quilt along all piecing seams.

3. Quilt around each image.

4. Quilt a triangle within each of the eight triangular blocks.

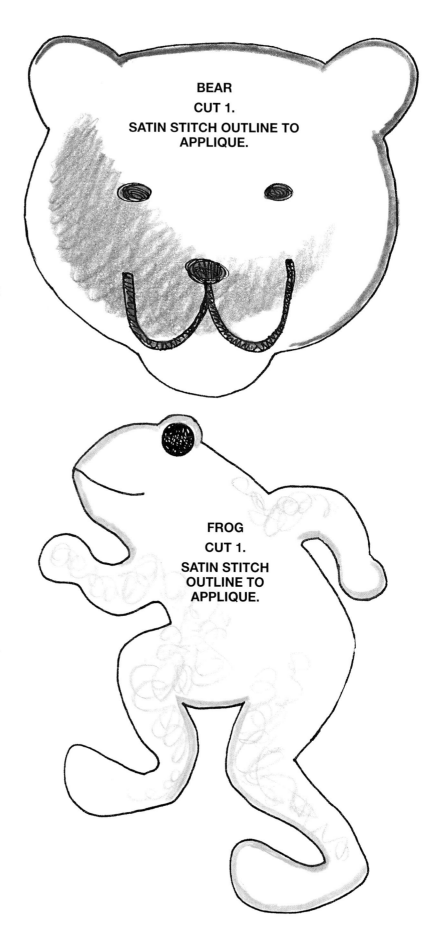

BEAR
CUT 1.
SATIN STITCH OUTLINE TO APPLIQUE.

FROG
CUT 1.
SATIN STITCH OUTLINE TO APPLIQUE.

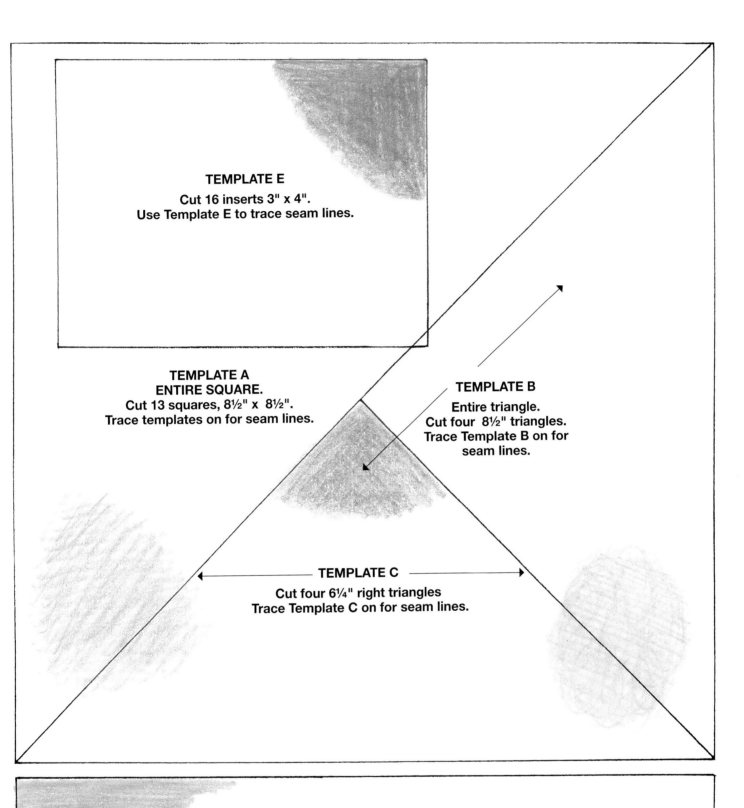

TEMPLATE E

Cut 16 inserts 3" x 4".
Use Template E to trace seam lines.

**TEMPLATE A
ENTIRE SQUARE.**
Cut 13 squares, 8½" x 8½".
Trace templates on for seam lines.

TEMPLATE B

Entire triangle.
Cut four 8½" triangles.
Trace Template B on for
seam lines.

TEMPLATE C

Cut four 6¼" right triangles
Trace Template C on for seam lines.

TEMPLATE D

Template to mark seam allowances for orange sashing.

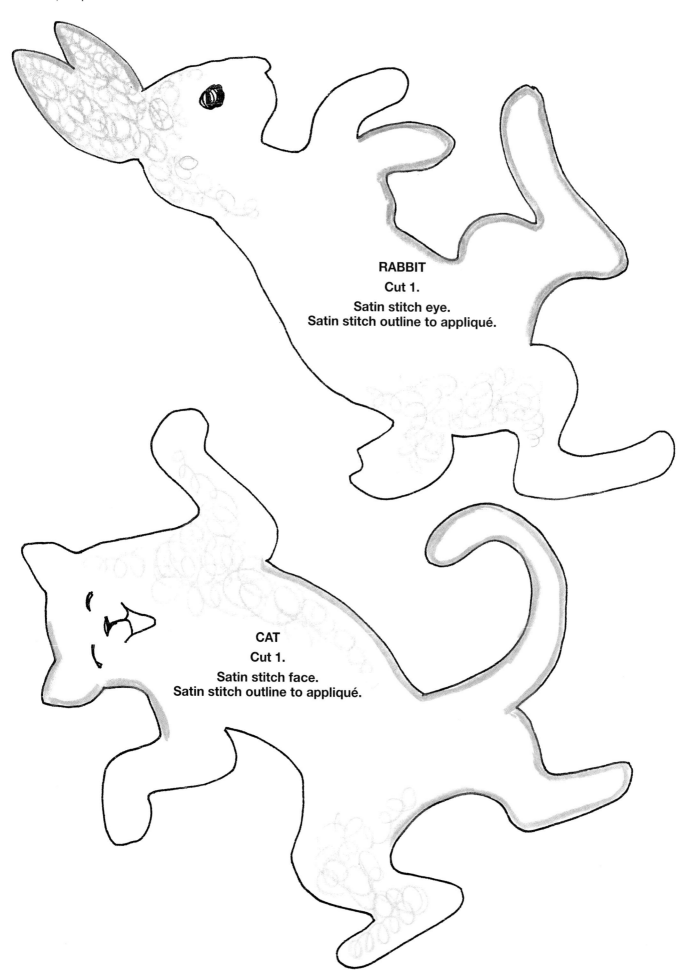

RABBIT

Cut 1.

Satin stitch eye.
Satin stitch outline to appliqué.

CAT

Cut 1.

Satin stitch face.
Satin stitch outline to appliqué.

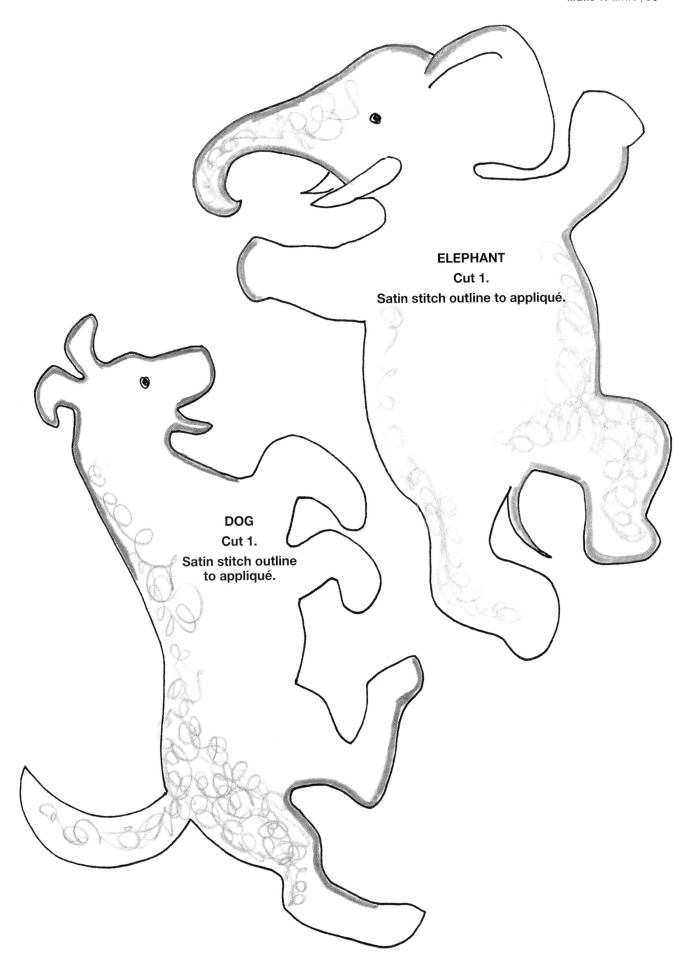

ELEPHANT
Cut 1.
Satin stitch outline to appliqué.

DOG
Cut 1.
Satin stitch outline
to appliqué.

Decorate-It Pillows

Materials

FABRIC

½ yard of fabric that coordinates with picture for pillow back

¼ yd. each of two or three fabrics that coordinate with picture

12" x 12" scrap of tight-weave white or light-colored poly-cotton

STUFFING AND BATTING

16" pillow form, or enough loose fiberfill to stuff a pillow

EMBELLISHMENTS AND NOTIONS

Threads to coordinate with border and backing fabric

TOOLS AND SUPPLIES

Packet of fabric or transfer crayons

Printer or typing paper

Iron and ironing board

Brush

Scissors

Sewing machine or serger

Pins

Get the kids involved with this quick and easy project, which also offers a great way to feature their artwork.

Kids of any age can draw with textile transfer crayons on plain paper, then get an adult to help iron the drawing onto plain fabric and sew the pillow. As you can tell from the pillow drawings, these kids were different ages. The Hot Stuff artist is 16, the rocket ship artist is 14, and a 7-year-old drew Batman and The Hulk.

Use textile or transfer crayons to make the drawing on plain white paper. This allows for experiments and rejects. When the right drawing is achieved, iron and set it onto the fabric, following the directions on the crayons used.

Drawings can be combined. Cut out the parts that you want, arrange them collage style, then iron them in place. Be inventive. You always can make another drawing if it doesn't turn out well.

To complete the pillow top, choose coordinating fabrics. The Log Cabin-style piecing used for the border on some of the pillows works well because you need not be as accurate as you would need to with other piecing techniques. The triangle border used on the Hulk pillow requires more accuracy in piecing. Once your border is attached to your drawing, sew on a backing fabric, turn and stuff the pillow, and sew the opening closed.

Draw

1. Lay a piece of typing or printer paper on a smooth surface.

2. Draw your design, using the fabric or transfer crayons. Remember, images will be reversed. Most boxes of fabric crayons contain only a handful of the colors typically available in paper crayons, so you will need to be inventive and combine colors to get the look you want.

3. Brush off little bits of crayon with a soft brush as you work to prevent the bits and crayon dust from transferring to your final drawing. Avoid brushing the crayon bits onto your ironing board cover.

4. If lettering is part of your design, draw it in reverse. Draw or copy lettering onto a separate sheet of white paper, flip the copied letters over, trace the reversed lettering onto a new sheet of paper, and finish the letters. For better visibility, use a light box or a day-lit windowpane to trace the lettering.

TIP: Use a day-lit window to help you trace letters.

Transfer

1. Iron the 12" x 12" square of white or light-colored poly-cotton fabric on an ironing board or a well-padded surface that can accept the heat of the iron.

2. Position the finished drawing in the center of the ironed fabric square. This allows for centering the drawing as you cut the block down to whatever size you wish after ironing on the design.

3. Pin the edges of the positioned drawing to the fabric to prevent shifting during the transfer process. You can use more than one drawing on a piece. Combine drawings, trim them to size so none overlap, and pin them in place on the fabric.

4. Place a scrap piece of paper under the drawing and fabric to blot extra color when ironed.

5. Using high heat, press the drawing onto the fabric. Set the iron on the drawing and fabric layers. Hold it in place briefly until the color on the drawing back shows through. Colors will be brighter after ironing. Avoid sliding the iron; that may move the drawing around and cause the image to print twice.

The iron's heat will transfer the drawing onto the fabric.

Cut

YOU WILL NEED THE FOLLOWING PATTERN PIECES: Template for Triangles (optional)

● **DRAWN BLOCK**

1. Measure and mark how much of the fabric printed with the finished drawing will show on the pillow front. On the pillows shown, the drawing blocks measured between 7½" and 8½" wide and 8" and 9¼" tall.

2. Draw a seam line on the back of the drawing block to the finished size.

3. Measure ½" seam allowance around the drawing block.

4. Cut off any extra fabric from the drawing block.

Sew and Stuff

1. Iron the border strips and the pillow backing.

2. Align the first border strip with the right edge of the drawing block, right sides together.

3. Sew the strip in place.

4. Press the seam to the darker-colored fabric to avoid shadowing. These seams are less likely to pull open and make it easier to assemble quilt pieces.

5. Repeat Steps 2 through 4 for the left, top and bottom edges of the drawing block. Be sure seams extend past the block through the edges, and clip off any extra side strip ends before opening and pressing the seams.

6. Keep adding longer and longer strips as desired to the outside edges. Alternate among the sides, top and bottom until you have a full-sized pillow.

7. Press the pillow face.

8. Match backing fabric to the finished pillow front, right sides together, and pin in place.

9. Sew backing fabric to the pillow front. Leave a 9" opening on one side.

10. Turn the pillow.

11. Insert the pillow form or fiberfill.

12. Sew the opening closed.

Iron the finished pillow face before completing the pillow.

● BORDER

1. Calculate the size of the border you will need to make a finished 16" x 16" pillow. Be sure to allow ¼" seam allowances for each piece to be sewn. I used between one and three strips for each pillow's Log Cabin-style border. Presewn strip widths ranged from 2" to 3½".

2. Cut or tear the desired number of border strips. On Log Cabin-style piecing, the strip widths need to be accurately measured, but the lengths can be random because they are trimmed off with each added piece.

Option: You also can piece triangles for a variation on the border.

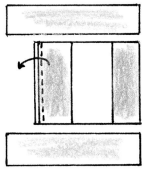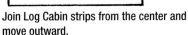

Join Log Cabin strips from the center and move outward.

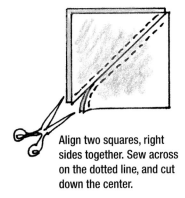

Align two squares, right sides together. Sew across on the dotted line, and cut down the center.

Join triangle squares into strips. Join strips to center block.

● BACKING

1. From the ½ yd. of coordinating fabric cut a 17" x 17" square for the pillow backing.

2. Mark ½" seam allowances on the pillow backing.

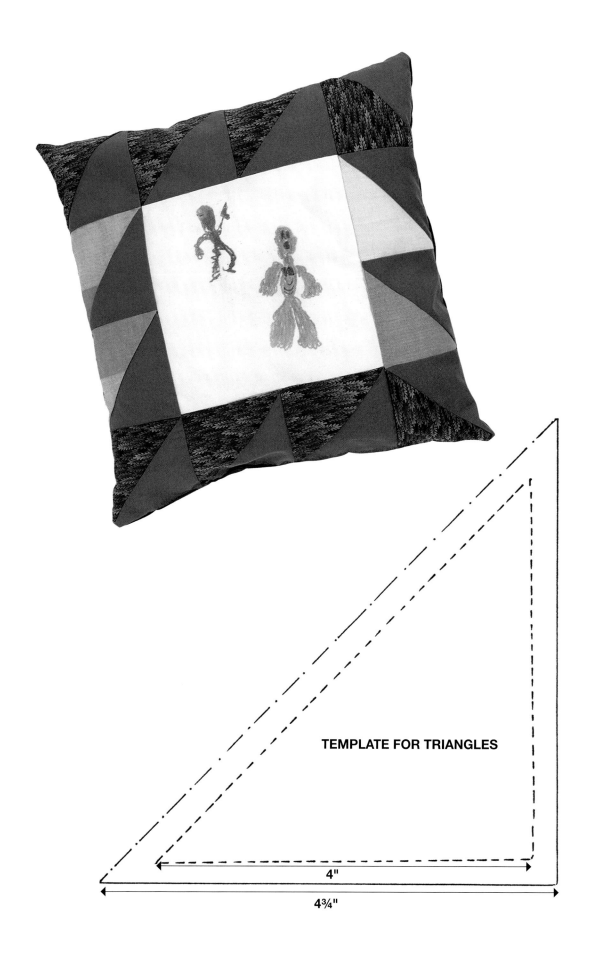

TEMPLATE FOR TRIANGLES

4"

4¾"

Story Quilts

The bedtime story is a wonderful family tradition. Snuggled in bed or cuddled in a lap, children learn the lore of their culture from the stories they are read or told.

"The Three Little Pigs" was my favorite book as a child. Perched on my grandfather's lap, I would read him the story while he helped me with the words. It never occurred to me that he already knew the story.

One of our kids' favorite books had split pages to make different combinations of images. And nursery rhymes offer another way to meet traditional characters. All of these literary characters provide inspiration for the quilts in this chapter.

CHAPTER

5

Puppet Quilt

Materials

FABRIC
1¾ yd. of 44" wide green fleece

1½ yd. of 44" wide white fleece

½ yd. of 44" wide cream fleece

⅓ yd. of 44" wide yellow fleece

⅓ yd. gray fleece

8" x 12" scrap of gold cotton print

8" x 12" scrap of brown cotton print

8" x 12" scrap of rust cotton plaid print

8" x 8" scrap of polka dot green cotton

6" x 9" scrap of lime green cotton checked print

4" x 12" scrap of gray faux fur, with ½" pile

2" x 3" scrap of pink felt

EMBELLISHMENTS AND NOTIONS
Large wad of fiberfill stuffing for puppets

½ yd. double-sided fusible web

Threads in black and white

Brown embroidery floss

2 post-and-washer toy eyes, ⅜" size

Tear-away stabilizer (optional)

TOOLS AND SUPPLIES
Sharp scissors

Pins

Iron and ironing board

Large-eye embroidery needle

Sharp hand sewing needle

Sewing machine

Pencil

When we were children, our mother acted out "The Three Little Pigs" for us. She would plop us three kids in chairs — our pig houses — and huff and puff as the Big Bad Wolf. We'd shriek in delighted terror and even convince the dog that we were in peril. This quilt savors that memory.

The puppet pigs and wolf are sewn into the blanket so a napping child can play out the scene alone, or mom, dad or a friend can join in.

Fleece does not yet come in every color in every store, so I used a just-right green fabric that featured embroidered shamrocks and worked the scene over and around the embroidery. Use whatever good shade of green you can find and key the added pieces to it so all the colors sing together.

This quilt is made double with white fleece on the back. However, it would take very close quilting of the layers to make it lie smooth. To compensate for this, I made random stitch lines that meander among the shamrocks. You also can make the quilt from a single layer of heavyweight fleece.

Cut

YOU WILL NEED THE FOLLOWING PATTERN PIECES: Pig Body, Pig Front, Pig Ear, Pig Tail, Wolf Body, Wolf Front, Wolf Muzzle, Wolf Ruff, Wolf Nose, Wolf Ear, Wolf Tail, Wolf Chin, Wolf Ruff Neck, Straw House, Straw House Chimney, Straw House Door, Stick House, Stick House Chimney, Stick House Door, Brick House, Brick House Roof, Brick House Chimney, Brick House Door, Brick House Door Window, Brick House Window, Small Tree, Large Tree, Grass

Note: Some patterns are given on the fold to save space. Cut the fabrics out on the fold, or for greater accuracy, cut one side singly, then flip the pattern and cut the other side.

1. From the green fleece cut one 44" x 56" piece for the quilt front.

2. From the white fleece cut one 44" x 48" piece for the quilt back, one Wolf Muzzle and one Wolf Chin.

3. From the yellow fleece cut one 10" x 44" strip for the quilt back trim piece.

4. From the cream fleece cut three Pig Bodies, three Pig Tails, six Pig Ears and three Pig Fronts. If you want lined ears, cut six Pig Ears from the pink felt. You will need to increase the pink felt on the materials list.

5. From the pink felt cut out six ½" circles for the Pig Eyes.

6. From the gray fleece cut out one Wolf Body, one Wolf Nose, one Wolf Front and four Wolf Ears (two in reverse).

7. From the gray fur fabric cut out one Wolf Tail, one Wolf Ruff Neck and one Wolf Ruff.

8. From the gold cotton print cut out one Straw House, one Brick House Window, One Brick House Door Window and one Stick House Door.

9. From the brown cotton print cut one Straw House Chimney, one Straw House Door, two Brick House Roofs and one Stick House.

10. From the rust cotton plaid print cut one Brick House, one Brick House Chimney and one Stick House Chimney.

11. From the lime green cotton checked print cut four Small Trees and one Large Tree.

12. From the green polka dot print cut three Grasses.

Appliqué

1. Test your fleece to see if it can withstand the ironing heat needed to fuse appliqué pieces. If it can, trace the various House, Tree and Grass patterns in reverse on double-sided fusible web. If not, cut out the House, Tree and Grass appliqué pieces and pin them in place.

TIP: Fleece shifts readily, so use pins liberally to secure appliqué pieces.

2. Follow the diagram and position the Houses, Trees and Grass on the green fleece.

3. Depending on the fleece's heat tolerance, iron or pin the House, Trees and Grass to the green fleece.

4. Satin stitch the House, Trees and Grass appliqués in place.

5. Use basting stitches to mark where the pigs and wolf will be sewn on the green fleece. Avoid using straight pins because they might fall out with all of the handling involved in creating this quilt.

6. Iron or pin the House Windows, Chimneys and Doors in place.

7. Straight stitch around each added piece first, then satin stitch the pieces' edges to secure them. If a test piece shows the satin stitching is pulling the fabric, use tear-away stabilizer paper on the back of the quilt.

Sew

● QUILT BACK AND FRONT

1. Quilt a brick pattern on the brick house.

2. Sew the yellow fleece header strip to the white quilt backing.

TIP: To skip this step, use an all-white backing that measures 44" x 56".

---

3. Spread out white fleece backing flat with its right side up.

4. Place the green quilt face right side down on top of the white fleece backing.

5. Smooth out the quilt face, then match and pin the edges of the quilt face and backing together. Use a seven-inch plate or other circle as a template to make the rounded corners.

6. Sew around the entire quilt leaving an 8" opening at the bottom for turning.

7. Trim the seam allowances.

8. Turn the quilt.

9. Sew a random quilting pattern to join the layers. Because the fleece shifts, expect the quilting to wrinkle somewhat.

● PIG PUPPETS

Note: These puppets were hand sewn with a tight overcast stitch, but you can machine sew them with a ⅛" seam if you like. If sewing this narrow seam is a problem, use the patterns as templates, adding a ¼" seam allowance all around and sew with a ¼" seam allowance.

1. Align the Pig Head and sew from the snout to the ear slot.

2. Sew from the Ear Slot to the back fold.

3. Match the Ear Slot edges.

4. Align two Pig Ears. Seam and turn. Repeat.

5. Fold a Pig Ear lengthwise as marked, tuck it into an ear slot, then pin it in place.

6. Turn the Pig Head right side out to ensure that the ears are at the proper angle. Turn the Pig Head back, then sew across the Ear Slot, including the Ears in the seam.

7. Align the Pig Front arms with the Pig Body arms; pin in place.

8. Match the bottom edges of the Pig Front and Pig Body; pin in place.

9. Match the Front Snout Tip with the Head Snout seam; pin in place.

10. Sew the Pig from the bottom edge around the entire Front.

11. Turn the Pig right side out.

12. Seam the Pig Tail, then sew it on as marked.

13. Repeat Steps 1 through 12 for the remaining Pigs.

● WOLF PUPPET

1. Fold the Wolf Body, right sides together. Sew the neck seam.

2. Align the Wolf Ruff to the Wolf Body, right sides together. Sew. Match the Wolf Ruff to the Wolf Front. Sew.

Making the pig puppets

Ear

Sew from the Snout to the Ear Slot.

Fold an Ear. Tuck it into an Ear Slot.

Sew the pig from the bottom edge around the entire Front.

Turn the finished puppet right side out. Add the Tail.

Embellish

3. Match the chin to the Wolf Ruff. Sew.

4. Sew the Wolf Nose to the Wolf Head. Fold the Wolf Head, and sew the Wolf Head nose seam.

5. Match the Nose seam to the Nose tip. Pin. Sew from the Wolf Eye to the nose to the other eye.

6. Match Ear front and back pieces. Sew, then turn.

7. Fold the Wolf Ear forward as marked and pin to the head on marks. Match the Head to the Ruff, right sides together, and sew.

8. Align the Wolf Front bottom corners, Arms, and Chin to the Wolf Body bottom corners, Arms, and nose seam. Sew from one bottom corner to the other to join. Turn the Wolf right side out.

9. Fold the Wolf Tail, right sides together, and sew (if the faux fur is too thick, sew the tail right side out). Sew the tail, right side out, as marked on Wolf Body.

● PIG PUPPETS

1. Use brown embroidery floss to sew the Pig's Mouth.

2. Use the brown floss to sew two French knots for the pig nostrils.

3. Push a 3" wad of stuffing into the Pig Snout and Head.

4. Sew through the stuffing to the Eye placement.

5. Sew on the pink Pig Eye with brown floss, making a large French knot in the center.

6. Sew across to the other Eye through the stuffing to hold it in place.

7. Sew on the second pink Pig Eye. Sew back into the Pig Head. Knot the thread under the eye patch.

8. Push a 2" wad of stuffing into the Pig Hoof.

9. Use brown thread to sew a groove into each hoof. Sew through the stuffing, and pull tightly to draw hooves together. Sew a knot to finish.

10. Repeat Steps 1 through 9 for the remaining Pig puppets.

● WOLF PUPPET

1. For a post-and-washer eye, insert the post. Push on the washer. Another option is to use felt circle eyes, finished with brown French knot centers, as was done on the Pig puppets.

2. Use brown embroidery floss to sew a mouth on the Wolf head.

● ATTACH PUPPETS

1. For each puppet, cut a hole through both layers of fleece that is the size of the puppet base.

2. Fit a puppet to each hole, making sure that the Pigs face their Houses and the Wolf.

3. Hand or machine sew each puppet to its corresponding hole. Be sure to sew through both layers. Sew firmly, as the puppets may get a lot of wear.

Making the wolf puppet

Align the Wolf Ruff and Body.

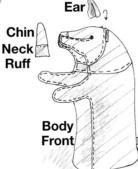

Add the Wolf Chin and Ears.

Turn the finished puppet right side out. Add the Tail.

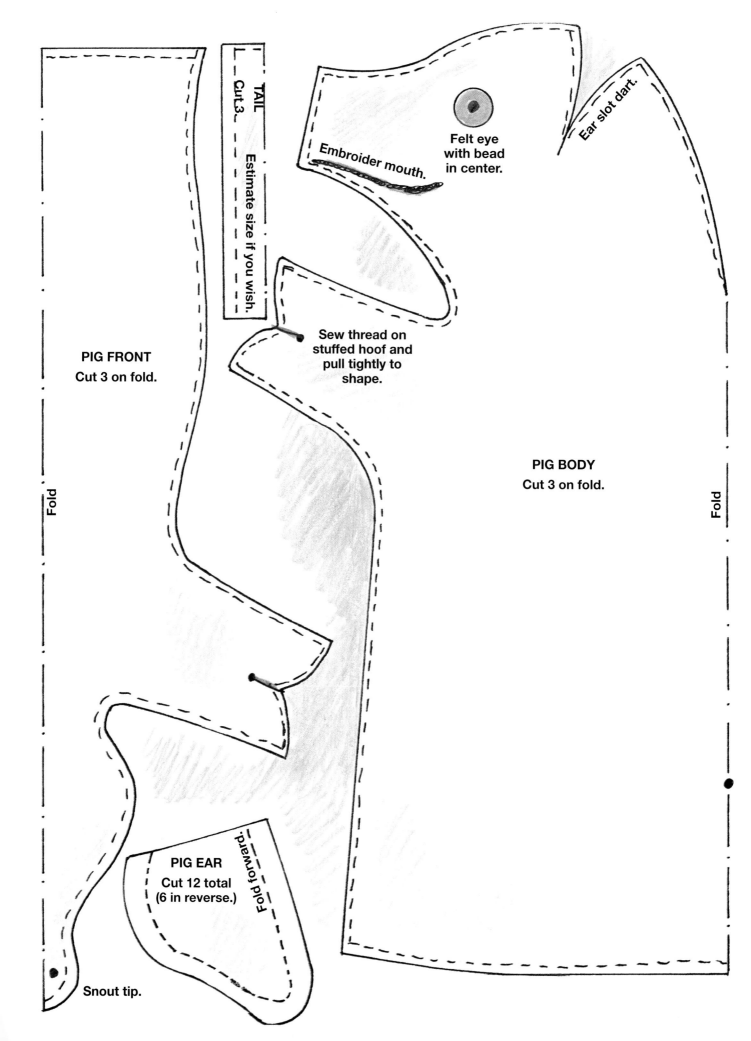

TAIL
Cut 3.

Estimate size if you wish.

PIG FRONT
Cut 3 on fold.

Fold

Embroider mouth.

Felt eye
with bead
in center.

Ear slot dart.

Sew thread on
stuffed hoof and
pull tightly to
shape.

PIG BODY
Cut 3 on fold.

Fold

PIG EAR
Cut 12 total
(6 in reverse.)

Fold forward.

Snout tip.

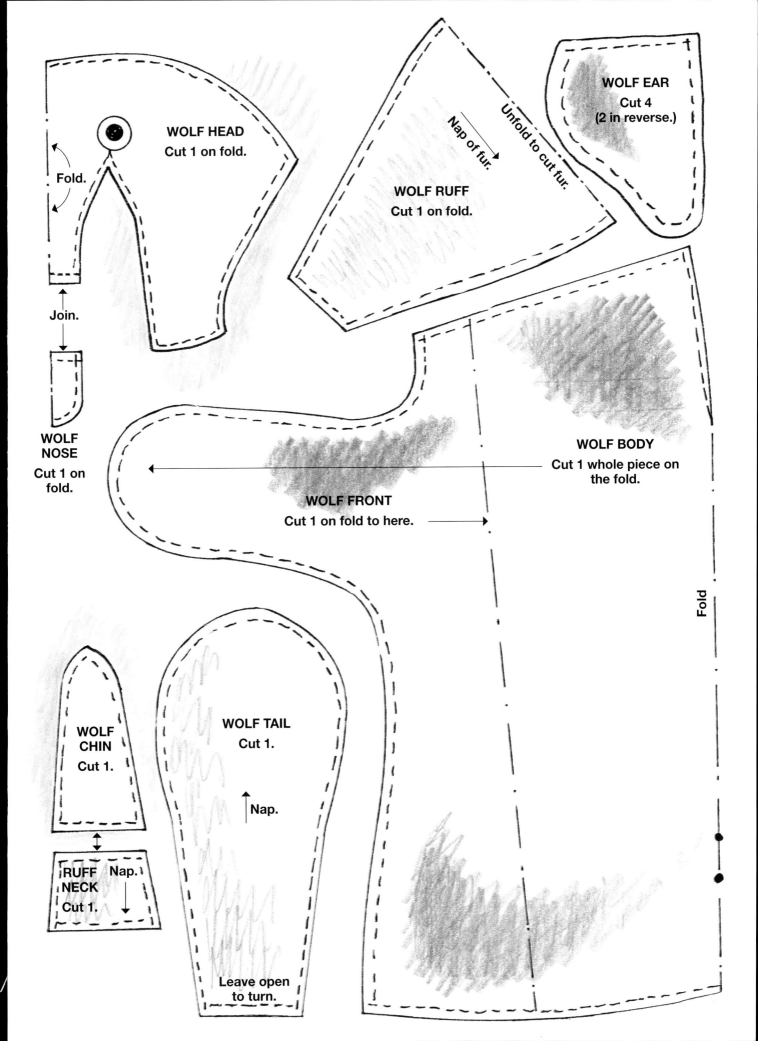

WOLF HEAD
Cut 1 on fold.

Fold.

Join.

WOLF
NOSE
Cut 1 on
fold.

Nap of fur.

Unfold to cut fur.

WOLF EAR
Cut 4
(2 in reverse.)

WOLF RUFF
Cut 1 on fold.

WOLF BODY
Cut 1 whole piece on
the fold.

WOLF FRONT
Cut 1 on fold to here.

Fold

WOLF
CHIN
Cut 1.

WOLF TAIL
Cut 1.

Nap.

RUFF
NECK
Cut 1.

Nap.

Leave open
to turn.

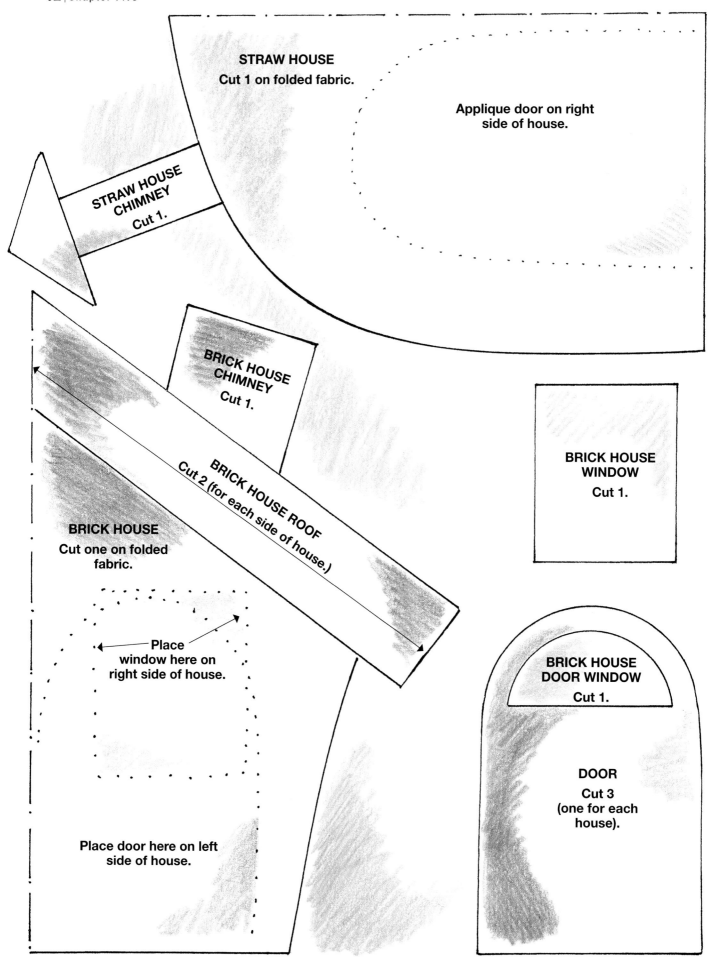

STRAW HOUSE
Cut 1 on folded fabric.

Applique door on right side of house.

STRAW HOUSE CHIMNEY
Cut 1.

BRICK HOUSE CHIMNEY
Cut 1.

BRICK HOUSE ROOF
Cut 2 (for each side of house.)

BRICK HOUSE WINDOW
Cut 1.

BRICK HOUSE
Cut one on folded fabric.

Place window here on right side of house.

BRICK HOUSE DOOR WINDOW
Cut 1.

DOOR
Cut 3 (one for each house).

Place door here on left side of house.

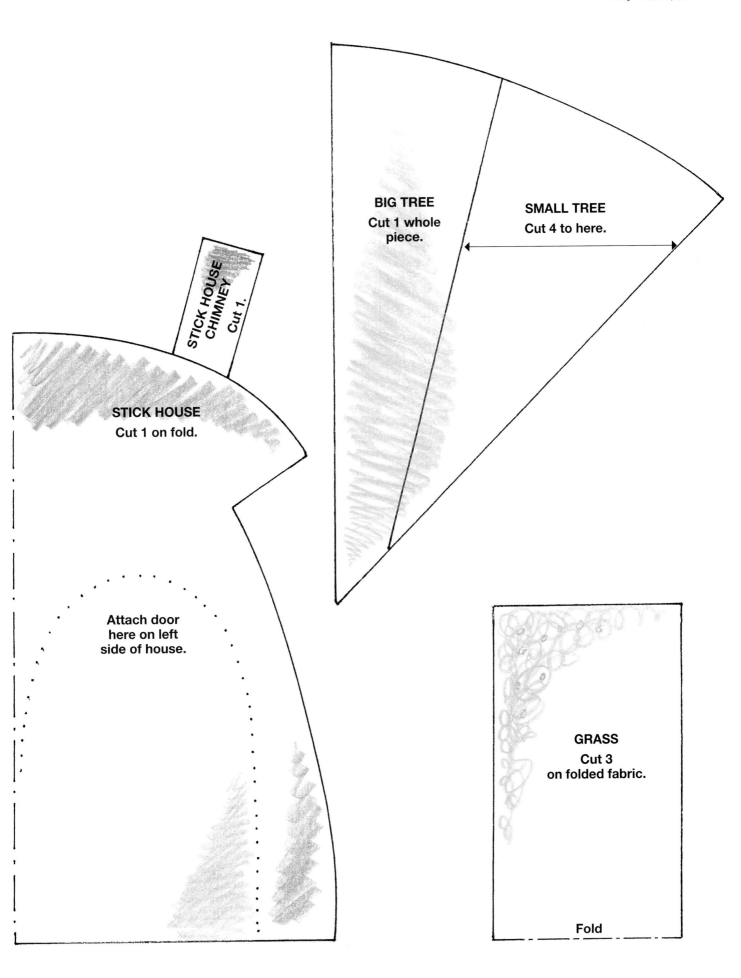

STICK HOUSE
CHIMNEY
Cut 1.

BIG TREE
Cut 1 whole
piece.

SMALL TREE
Cut 4 to here.

STICK HOUSE
Cut 1 on fold.

Attach door
here on left
side of house.

GRASS

Cut 3
on folded fabric.

Fold

Scrambled People

Materials

FABRIC

2½ yd. 44" wide blue-green spatter print poly cotton

1 yd. of 42" wide white duck cloth

¼ yd. brown poly-cotton

9" x 9" lavender star print polyester

8" x 12" peach poly-cotton

8" x 8" scrap of small orange plaid

6" x 8" scrap of blue denim-colored fabric

6" x 8" scrap of tan fabric

3" x 3" scrap of green checked print

2" x 3" scrap of gold tissue polyester

EMBELLISHMENTS AND NOTIONS

37" x 46" quilt batting

5 yd. green 1" bias tape or quilt binding

36" strip of hook and loop tape, or 36 pairs of 1" wide precut hook and loop tape closures

Double-sided fusible web

Threads in white, purple, orange, green and dark green

TOOLS AND SUPPLIES

Sharp scissors

Paper for pattern

Yardstick

No. 2 pencil

Iron and ironing board

Sewing machine

Serger (optional)

Quilting pins

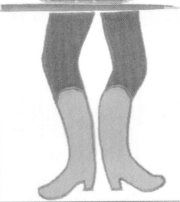

In our bookcase is an old family favorite, a book whose pages split into three sections to let you make different combination pictures.

Our kids and grandkids have enjoyed this book, which is evident by the well-worn edges. This quilt is based on that dear old book, except that the "pages" are blocks of appliquéd fabric with hook and loop tape on their backs.

The book was bound, so the choices were limited. But children can place the nine blocks anywhere on this quilt for whatever bizarre combinations might appeal to them.

Kids can play with this 35" x 42" quilt flat, but there also is a rod pocket in the top to allow the scene to work as a wall hanging in a child's room. If you use this as a wall hanging, hang it low enough so the child can easily reach all the pieces.

The heavy canvas duck fabric used for the appliquéd blocks is stiff enough to prevent the satin stitching on the appliqués from pulling. Duck fabric is cumbersome to sew, so I serged the edges to avoid making corners.

Cut and Fuse

YOU WILL NEED THE FOLLOWING PATTERN PIECES FROM THE PULLOUT: Horse's Head, Horse's Body, Horse's Legs, Dancer's Head, Dancer's Body, Dancer's Legs, Cowboy's Head, Cowboy's Body, Cowboy's Legs, Block Template

● QUILT

1. From the blue-green spatter print cut two 37" x 44" pieces, one for the quilt front and the other for the quilt back. The quilt's finished size will be 34" x 41", including a rod pocket at the top.

2. From the quilt batting cut one 36" x 44" piece for the quilt filling.

● APPLIQUE PATTERNS

1. Make two copies of each of the pattern blocks. Set aside one set to serve as a construction guide later. From the other set, cut out all of the detailed pieces, including faces, hands, gloves, boots, hairlines, kerchief pieces, hair, crown, star, dress, shirt, hat and pants.

2. Group pattern pieces according to the color of fabric on which they will be appliquéd.

> **Brown poly-cotton:** Dancer's Hair, Horse's Body, Horse's Legs and Horse Head.
> **Lavender star print:** Dancer's Dress.
> **Peach poly-cotton:** Dancer's Face, Cowboy's Face, Dancer's Legs and Dancer's Arms.
> **Orange plaid:** Cowboy's Shirt.
> **Green checked print:** Cowboy's Kerchief.
> **Blue denim-colored fabric:** Cowboy's Jeans.
> **Tan fabric:** Cowboy's Boots, Hat and Gloves.
> **Gold tissue polyester:** Dancer's Crown and Cowboy's Star.

3. Cluster pattern pieces in reverse on the fusible web. Arrange pieces into color-matched units.

4. Trace each group of reversed pattern pieces on the reverse side of the fusible web. The reverse side of fusible web is the side on which your pencil works best.

5. Cut apart color-matched pattern clusters.

6. Iron each pattern cluster onto the reverse side of its corresponding fabric.

7. Cut out the individual fused appliqué pieces. Wait to peel off the backing paper until you are ready to iron the pieces onto their blocks.

● DUCK CLOTH BLOCKS

1. Copy and cut out the Block Template.

2. From the white duck cloth cut nine 9" x 18" pieces for the quilt blocks.

3. Fold a 9" x 18" duck cloth rectangle in half.

4. With the folded edge to the top, draw the hook and loop tape placement templates on the back side of the block. Use the Block Template as a guide.

5. On the top fold, draw the figure placement as marked on the corresponding pattern block.

6. Starting 8" down from the top fold, mark where the figures will meet as shown on each pattern block. On the row of appliqué heads, figures align along the bottom edge at the block at 8". On the bottom row of legs, figures align along the top edge.

7. Repeat Steps 3 through 6 for remaining blocks.

● QUILT GRID

1. From the bias tape cut two strips measuring 30" apiece and two strips measuring 26 " apiece.

2. Leave the rest of the bias tape uncut.

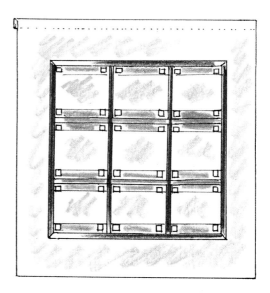

Appliqué

1. Align the fused Dancer's Dress appliqué piece to the top edge marks and the bottom marks on the block. Iron the dress firmly in place.

2. Match a second folded block to the bottom edge of the dress, aligning the block's top edge with the bottom edge of the Dancer's Dress.

3. Match the Dancer's Legs to both the template marks on the block and the Dancer's Dress. Iron in place.

4. Match the Dancer's Dress block to the Dancer's Head block, which is folded 8" down on the block. Align the neck to the template marks. Iron on the Dancer's face, hair and crown pieces.

5. Unfold the appliquéd blocks to sew a single duck cloth layer.

6. With orange thread, satin stitch around each appliqué piece on all three blocks to secure pieces in place and provide an outline, then satin stitch the features.

7. Repeat Steps 1 through 6 for the Cowboy appliqués. Use green thread to satin stitch the appliqué edges and details.

8. Repeat Steps 1 through 6 for the Horse appliqués. Use purple thread to satin stitch the appliqué edges and details.

Satin stitched appliqué edges highlight details on the moveable panels.

Sew

● HOOK AND LOOP TAPE

1. Join a 36" strip of hook and loop tape together. Cut it into 1" pieces.

TIP: You also can use precut hook and loop tape segments, which would eliminate Step 1.

2. Separate the stiff hook pieces from the soft loop pieces. Set aside the soft pieces to use when you finish the quilt front.

3. Place a 1" hook patch in each corner of each block as marked. Machine stitch in place. Sew on the patch edges, then sew across from corner to corner for a secure hold.

● BLOCKS

1. Fold a block, right sides together, and align the bottom edges at the 8" mark.

2. Stitch a line on the bottom edge, ⅛" below the 8" mark. The finished blocks must measure 8" from top to bottom and 8½" from side to side. All blocks must be the same height and width.

3. Turn the block right side out.

4. Finish the block sides using a serger or an overcast stitch. If you prefer, you can use bias tape to bind the side edges rather than serging or overcast stitching. Or, if the cloth is flexible enough, you can seam the block sides. Just be sure to leave an opening to turn the block back out. The heavy duck I used was too stiff to turn or make good corners.

● QUILT

1. Lay the quilt front and back flat, with right sides together. Smooth the batting on top of the quilt fabric.

Option: You can use pre-quilted fabric to save time.

2. Pin the layers together along the edges, placing the pins across the seam line every 6".

3. Using a ½" seam allowance, sew around quilt to join all three layers. Leave an opening at the top of the quilt that is large enough to turn the quilt right side out.

4. Trim the seam allowances, removing as much batting from the seam allowances as possible. Clip across the corners to lessen the bulk.

5. Turn the quilt right side out, using care to completely open the seams.

6. Press the edges.

7. Sew the opening closed.

8. Turn over a 2" hem at the top of the quilt for a rod pocket.

9. Topstitch the rod pocket in place.

● GRID

1. Measure 7" down from the top of the quilt and 12" in from the left edge. Pin one of the 30" bias tape strips in place vertically so the left edge of the tape is on the 12" mark and the top of the tape is at the 7" mark.

2. Measure 7" down from the top of the quilt and 12" in from the right edge of the quilt. Pin one of the 30" bias tape strips in place vertically so the right edge of the tape is on the 12" mark and the top of the tape is at the 7" mark.

3. Measure 17" up from the bottom of the quilt and 2" from the left edge of the quilt. Pin one of the 26" bias tape strips in place horizontally so the bottom edge of the tape is on the 17" mark and the left edge of the tape is at the 2" mark.

4. Measure 17" down from the top of the quilt and 2" from the right edge of the quilt. Pin one of the 26" bias tape strips in place horizontally so the top edge of the tape is on the 17" mark and the left edge of the tape is at the 2" mark.

TIP: The finished series of strips should resemble a Tic Tac Toe board and mark off nine equal sections.

5. Check that the grid strips are aligned correctly by placing the finished blocks on the quilt. Reposition any strips if necessary. The vertical strips will be more visible than the horizontal ones.

6. Measure 7" down from the top of the quilt and 2" in from the left edge. Starting at the left edge, pin the uncut length of bias tape and run it straight across the quilt until it is 2" away from the right edge of the quilt. The uncut bias tape should cover the edges of the vertical strips beneath it.

7. At the right end, fold a mitered corner in the strip. Pin in place.

8. Staying 2" away from the right edge of the quilt, run the uncut bias tape down the quilt for a length of 26"; pin tape periodically. The uncut tape should cover the edges of the horizontal grid pieces.

9. Fold and pin a second mitered corner on the bias tape.

10. Measure 7" up from the bottom of the quilt and 2" in from the right edge. Run the uncut bias tape straight across the quilt, pinning periodically, until the strip is 2" away from the left edge of the quilt. The uncut tape should cover the edges of the vertical strips beneath it.

11. Fold and pin a third mitered corner on the bias tape.

12. Run the uncut bias tape up the quilt, staying 2" away from the left edge of the quilt. Pin it in place. Cut the tape where it is even with the top edge of the top horizontal strip. Fold an angled corner to complete the frame.

13. Topstitch the grid pieces in place. Sew ¹⁄₁₆" from the tape edge on both sides.

● HOOK AND LOOP TAPE

1. Position all of the 1" loop tape segments on the quilt front. One piece of tape should be in each corner of each grid block. Use the finished blocks as guides to ensure the tape segments line up.

2. Sew the edges of the tape, then sew across from corner to corner.

3. Attach appliquéd blocks to the quilt.

Humpty Dumpty
Pajama Holder

Materials

FABRIC
¾ yd. poly-cotton print

½ yd. eggshell fleece

⅓ yd. light blue fleece

10" x 14" scrap of pink and white striped cotton or poly-cotton fabric

6" x 12" scrap of bright pink poly-cotton

6" x 12" purple felt

4" x 16" scrap of light orange fleece

4" x 4" scrap of pink fleece or felt

EMBELLISHMENTS AND NOTIONS
24" x 32" piece of bonded fiberfill

1 white plastic 12" jacket zipper

1 green four-hole button

1 yellow four-hole button

2 blue four-hole buttons, or scraps of blue and black fleece (eyes)

Seam sealant

Threads in white (buttonhole and regular), purple and orange

TOOLS AND SUPPLIES
Newsprint or similar paper that will tear away easily

Pencil with eraser or ¼" dowel to turn project

Sewing machine

Pins

Scissors

Pencil

Humpty Dumpty is a favorite nursery rhyme character purported to be a British political figure who fell out of favor. The broken egg symbolizes Humpty's fall from grace, as "all the king's horses and all the king's men couldn't put Humpty together again."

That concept of political peril still resonates today. But in this project, Humpty passes up politics for pajamas. Zip open his mouth and shove your pajamas between all those white teeth.

I tried some risky techniques on this project. One was using a heavy jacket-type plastic zipper sewn into the curved mouth. The zipper definitely did not want to curve sideways.

The second risky thing was using fleece fabric. Fleece is a synthetic fabric that feels fluffy soft and frays very little when cut.

It also stretches and shifts when sewn by machine. With this fabric and a stiff zipper, the zipper will win... unless you line the fleece and add filler for quilting the egg face.

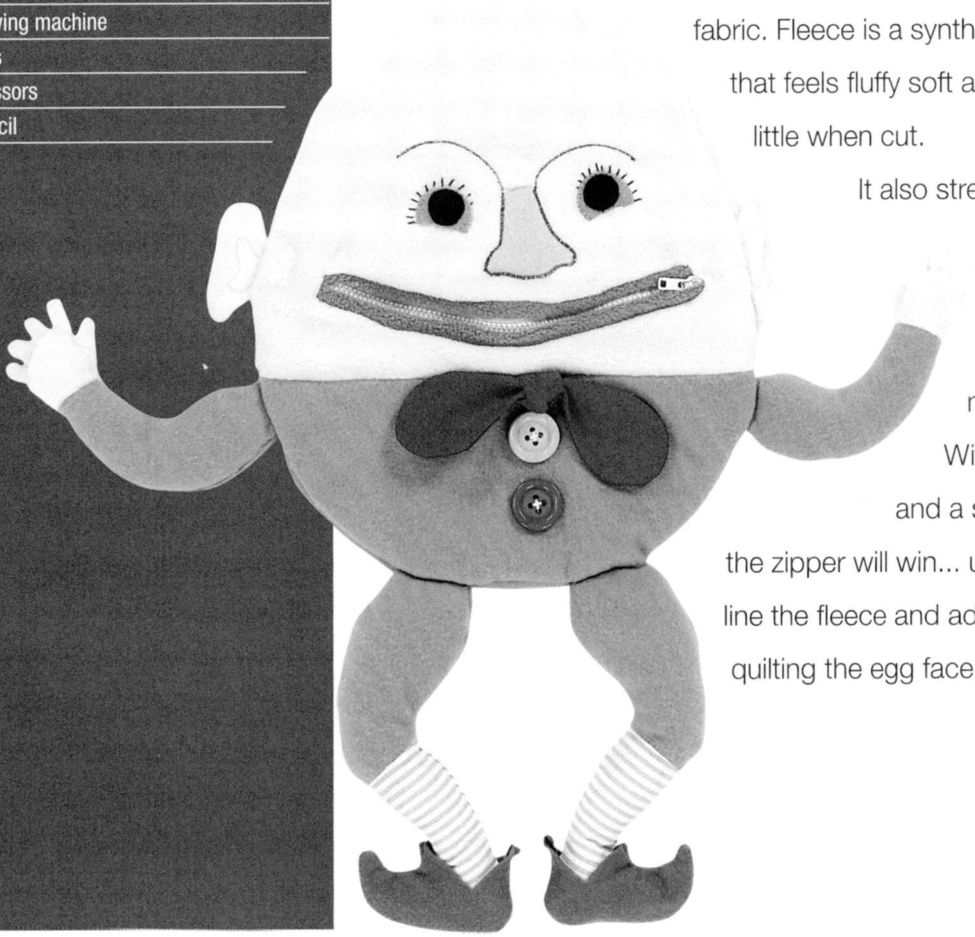

Cut

YOU WILL NEED THE FOLLOWING PIECES FROM THE PATTERN PULLOUT:
Egg Head, Egg Body, Thigh, Leg, Shoe, Arm, Tie, Lip, Hand, Ear

● PATTERNS

1. Trace two copies of the Hand on newsprint or other paper that will tear away easily.

2. Cut out the project pattern pieces from the pullout section.

● FABRIC

Note: Some pattern pieces will need to be traced in reverse.

1. From the eggshell fleece cut two Egg Heads (one reversed) and four Ears (two reversed.)

2. From the light blue fleece cut two Egg Bodies (one reversed), four Thighs (two reversed), and four Egg Arms (two reversed).

3. From the pink and white strip cut four Legs (two reversed).

4. From the purple felt cut four Shoes (two reversed).

5. From the bright pink fabric cut two Ties.

6. From the pink felt cut one Nose.

7. From the orange fleece cut two Lips. Optional cut: two cheek circles.

8. From the poly-cotton print, cut two Egg Bodies (one reversed) and two Egg Heads (one reversed.)

9. From the fiberfill cut two Egg Bodies (one reversed) and two Egg Heads (one reversed.)

The Humpty Dumpty character offers a place for kids to stash their pajamas.

Sew

● FRONT AND BACK

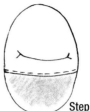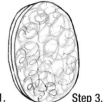

Step 1.   Step 3.

1. Match the Head and Body Front. Seam across.

2. Repeat Step 1 for the Head and Body Back.

3. Place the assembled Back right side down. Smooth on the filler, then place the lining on top, right side up.

4. Pin the Back, filler and lining layers together.
Note: You will wait to sew the Egg Front and Back together until the Assembly steps.

● ZIPPER MOUTH

Place the lining over the mouth.

1. Following the pattern, trace and cut the Mouth shape in the Egg Front, filler and lining layers.

2. Align the zipper face to face with the Upper Lip. Sew the Upper Lip and zipper together, sewing ⅛" from the zipper teeth.

3. Fold the Upper Lip right side out. The zipper teeth should show just below the lip. Pin or baste the Lip edge with the zipper edge.

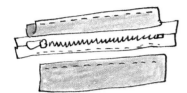

Sew the zipper mouth.

4. Align the Upper Lip raw edges with the Upper Mouth raw edges. Sew across, using a ¼" seam allowance.

The fleece will conform to the zipper.

5. Repeat Steps 2 through 4 for the Lower Lip. Although cut on a curve, the soft stretchy fleece will conform to the straight zipper at this point.

6. If the zipper ends look messy, appliqué orange cheek circles onto the face to cover them.

● FIBERFILL AND LINING

1. Working from the reverse side of the Head, align the Head Lining's curved lower edge with the Upper Lip/zipper raw edges. Pin at intervals, because the zipper will resist curving.

2. Stitch on the seam line to join the lining to the lip and head.

3. Lay the fiberfill on the Head lining.

4. Flip up the lining and fiberfill to align with the Egg Head, and pin the layers together. This encloses the zipper edge.

5. Sew the lining on the Lip/zipper/Head seam line.

6. Repeat Steps 1 through 5 to enclose the zipper edge for the Lower Lip/Body/Lower Head portion.

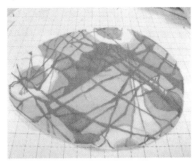

Line the inside of the pajama holder.

● FACE

1. Lightly mark the Eyebrows on the Egg Head front.

2. Position the Nose on the Egg Head front.

3. With orange thread and a machine satin stitch, sew one Eyebrow. Applique the left, bottom and right edges of the Nose. Sew the other Eyebrow in one continuous line.

4. Straight stitch across the top of the Nose.

5. Use a sturdy thread to sew the button eyes in place beneath the Eyebrows.
   Note: You also can use colored fleece and black felt to create custom eyes. Use the fleece for the irises and felt for the pupils. Stitch layers in place below the Eyebrows, then add a finishing touch by stitching black thread eyelashes. Photographs of this project show both examples.

● EARS

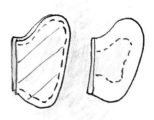

1. Match two fleece Ear pieces, right sides together.

2. Sew a ¼" seam around the edges.

3. Turn the Ear right side out. The seam allowance provides stuffing.

4. Topstitch the Ear pattern to quilt the ear.

5. Repeat Steps 1 through 4 for the other Ear.

● TIE

1. Match the Tie pieces.

2. Begin in the center and sew all around the tie, leaving a gap to turn the piece right side out.

3. Trim the seam allowances.

4. Turn the Tie right side out.

5. Sew the opening closed.

6. Tie the Tie in a knot. Sew it onto the Egg Front.

● LEGS

1. Match one Thigh and one Leg piece, right sides together.

2. Sew the pieces together at the knee seam.

3. Repeat Steps 1 and 2 for the three remaining pairs of leg pieces.

4. Match two joined Thigh and Leg pieces, right sides together, and sew, leaving the top of the thigh open.

5. Clip the seam allowances. Turn the Leg right side out.

6. Stuff the foot firmly with fiber-fill, and stuff the rest of the leg softly.

7. Repeat Steps 4 through 6 for the other assembled leg.

● SHOES

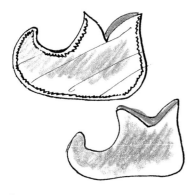

1. Match two Shoe pieces, right sides together.

2. Using matching thread, sew the seam with a narrow satin stitching.

3. Trim the seam allowance. Add seam sealant to the seam ends.

4. Turn right side out.

5. Repeat for the other Shoe.

6. Pull the shoes onto the character's feet.

● ARMS AND HANDS

1. Match Hand fabric to one Arm. Sew at the wrist to join the pieces.

2. Repeat Step 1 for the remaining Arm pieces.

3. Place the two matching Arm pieces right sides together. Pin, matching the wrist seams.

4. Pin the traced Hand pattern onto the Hand fabric as a stitch guide.

5. Begin at the shoulder to sew the arm. Carefully stitch the Hand on the paper pattern. Make a little square corner between the fingers as shown on the pattern.

6. Tear off the paper pattern. Trim the seam allowances.

7. Clip to the stitch line between the fingers.

8. Carefully turn the Hand and fingers using the eraser end of a pencil or a slightly sharpened ¼" dowel. Hold the Hand firmly to prevent the turning tool from poking through the fabric.

9. Stuff the arm lightly.

10. Repeat Steps 1 through 9 for the other Arm.

LEFT: Pin the tear-away paper pattern on the Hand fabric, then stitch in place.
RIGHT: Remove the paper pattern. Cut around the shape.

Assemble

1. Place each Ear on the Egg Front as marked. Align the raw edges. Pin in place.

2. Baste Ears in place.

3. Place the Arms on the Egg body, right sides together, with raw edges aligned. The Hands likely will cover the Eyes.

4. Baste the Arms in place.

5. Lay the Legs on the body, right sides together, with raw edges aligned.

6. Baste Legs in place.

7. Align the assembled Front with the assembled Back. Make sure that all added pieces are tucked and that the zipper is left partly open.

8. Sew around the edges of the assembled Egg Front and Back with a ¼" seam. Overcast stitch the edges if your wish. Sewing all these layers is difficult. You can leave the lining out of the seam, then sew the front and back linings together.

9. Trim any exposed seam allowances evenly.

10. Turn the Egg right side out through the unzipped mouth.

11. Hand sew the lining at the mouth corners.

Baste the arms and legs in place.

Wearable Quilts

Who hasn't worn a quilt at some time? Wrap it around yourself to be a robed king, pull it around your neck and leap off tall sofas to be a superhero, or drape it over sofa cushions to make a tent. Wearable quilts can fill hours of playtime.

Mitten Quilt

Materials

FABRIC

1 yd. fleece in snowflake or other print, 60" wide.

¾ yd. of light blue fleece, 60" wide

EMBELLISHMENTS AND NOTIONS

12" x 48" piece of fiberfill

Serger threads, or matching thread

TOOLS AND SUPPLIES

Sewing machine

Serger (optional)

Scissors

Marking pencil

Pins

Imagine a mitten big enough for a giant. The size of this mitten changes its function from keeping a hand warm to keeping an entire child warm. Just pop halfway into this bag and keep snuggly warm while watching TV.

Also, there is an old-time game to play with a super-sized mitten. Climb in, pull up the mitten, and hop to the starting line for a sack race. A smaller child can crawl inside the mitten and use it as a tent. It is fun to watch the shifting shapes of a mitten full of child. This project, when finished, measures 24" wide: The thumb is 10" x 12", and the total length is 42". This mitten is easy to make. Cozy fleece sews up easily, but you also can make this mitten of quilted cotton fabric, fur fabric or other heavy fabrics.

For extra warmth, make the mitten double.

Cut

YOU WILL NEED THE FOLLOWING PIECES FROM THE PATTERN PULLOUT: Curves A and B.

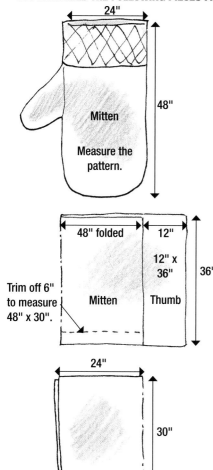

24"

48"

Mitten

Measure the pattern.

48" folded   12"

12" x 36"

36"

Trim off 6" to measure 48" x 30".

Mitten   Thumb

24"

30"

Use Curve A to cut the corners.

● MITTEN HAND

Note: This project is too large for a pattern to be included in the book, but you easily can measure and mark the mitten dimensions directly on the fabric. Use Curve A for the rounded corners.

1. Fold the 60" width of fleece over so it measures 24" from the selvage to the fold and 36" the length of the fold.

2. Cut the doubled-over layer of fleece so that the remaining single layer of fleece measures 10" x 36".

3. Set aside the 10" x 36" remnant for the Thumb.

4. Trim 6" off the top edge of the Hand fabric; it will now measure 48" x 30" unfolded.

5. Fold the Hand fabric to form a 24" x 30" rectangle. Use the Curve A guide to cut the two lower corners.

● MITTEN THUMB

1. Fold the fabric remnant in half lengthwise to measure 10" x 18".

2. Measure down 8" from the top on the cut edges.

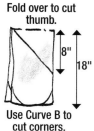

Fold over to cut thumb.

8"

18"

Use Curve B to cut corners.

3. Mark and cut a diagonal line through both layers of fabric from the fold top to the 8" mark. This line will be where the Thumb piece attaches to the Hand of the Mitten.

4. Using the Curve B pattern, cut the bottom edge of the fabric in a large curve.

5. From the light blue fleece, measure and cut a 24" x 48" cuff.

6. From the fiberfill, cut a 12" x 48" piece. The fiberfill is optional. The Mitten Cuff can be filled and quilted, or simply sewn.

Sew

● HAND

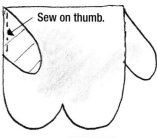

Sew on thumb.

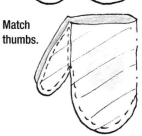

Match thumbs.

1. Align the diagonal cut edge of one Thumb with a matching edge of a Hand piece at the top edge. This will create an angled Thumb.

2. Position the aligned Thumb and Hand, right sides together.

3. Seam the Thumb and Hand using a serger, or use an overcast stitch on a regular sewing machine.

4. Repeat Steps 1 through 3 for the other Thumb and Hand pieces.

5. Align the two assembled Hands, right sides together, so the Thumb seams match.

6. Sew from the fold on the thumb to make a smooth curve.

7. Sew up the Thumb, down the Hand and around the Hand's bottom curves. Make a smooth ending on the fold.

Cut

● REGULAR CUFF

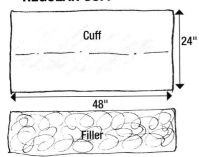

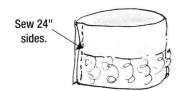

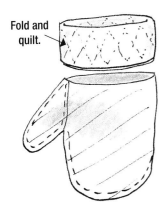

1. Fold the Cuff to match the 24" edges.

2. Seam the 24" edges together.

3. Turn the Cuff right side out, widthwise, with the seam inside.

4. Tuck the right-side-out Cuff into the unturned Mitten.

5. Align the Cuff side seam with the Thumb fold. Match the Cuff raw edges to the Mitten raw edges.

6. Serge or overcast the seam that connects the Mitten and Cuff.

7. Turn the finished Mitten right side out.

● QUILTED CUFF (OPTIONAL)

1. Position the lining on one side of the Cuff.

2. Match the Cuff's 24" edges together.

3. Seam the edges, including the fiberfill in this seam.

4. Trim the seam allowance.

5. Fold the Cuff lengthwise over the fiberfill so the seam is enclosed.

6. Quilt the Cuff. Quilting will shorten the Cuff's circumference. When you tuck it inside the Hand to join the pieces, the Hand's circumference will be larger. Take up the slack by pinning it to fit.

7. Pin the quilted Cuff to the unturned Hand.

8. Seam the Cuff and Hand together.

9. Turn the finished Mitten right side out.

Variation: Thicker mitten

If you want a doubly-thick Mitten, alter the directions throughout the project to include these steps.

1. Cut the Mitten and Thumb patterns double, or cut additional fabric to line the Mitten's Hand and Thumb.

2. Sew the Mitten pieces to the top and bottom edges of the Cuff.

3. Join all four Thumb pieces.

4. Sew around the Mitten, leaving the bottom edge of the lining Mitten open for 12".

5. Turn the Mitten right side out.

6. Align the top and bottom Cuff edges; topstitch in place.

7. Fold a hem in the lining Mitten's bottom edge.

8. Machine sew the opening in the lining Mitten closed.

Labels in figures: Cuff · 24" · 48" · Filler · Sew 24" sides. · Fold and quilt.

Dragon Quilt

Materials

FABRIC

2 yd. of reversible print metallic gold fabric, 42" wide

2 yd. red polyester fabric

1½ yd. navy blue fleece, 60" wide

1 yd. green metallic fabric

2" x 4" scrap of black felt

EMBELLISHMENTS AND NOTIONS

3 yd. paper-backed fusible web

24" x 24" piece of lightweight bonded batting

25mm plastic eyes

Threads in red, gold, green, black and navy

TOOLS AND SUPPLIES

Needle

Sharp scissors

Newsprint for the pattern

Glue gun

Glue sticks

Sewing machine

Serger (optional)

Iron and ironing board

6" Plate

When I was growing up, my dad would toss a blanket over the three of us kids, and we'd pretend to be a dragon. That dragon was imaginary; this pattern gives it form.

This quilt, which measures 54" by 60", features double-sided metallic woven fabric, which is ideal for shading the dragon's form, although it is more delicate than tabby-weave cotton fabrics.

This flexible fleece quilt will stretch as the kids play dragon, but the appliqué seams may pull out. To increase stability, use paper-backed fusible web on the gold fabric. Or, stabilize and embellish a plain fabric by topstitching loops for scales by free motion.

When using the double-sided fabric, flip selected pattern pieces. Create a shaded effect by using the darker reverse side of the metallic fabric for some pieces. If you plan to use a loosely woven fabric, trace each pattern piece in reverse onto the fusible web and iron it onto the corresponding fabric's wrong side, except for the Ruff and Head.

Although fusing fabrics is not recommended with fleece, it can succeed if you test the fleece for ironing first. Use the lowest possible heat setting for fusing, then use a pressing cloth to iron on the fused pieces from the quilt back, then appliqué them immediately.

Cut

YOU WILL NEED THE FOLLOWING PIECES FROM THE PATTERN PULLOUT: Right Top Leg, Right Bottom Leg, Left Top Leg, Left Bottom Leg, Left Body, Right Body Top, Lower Body, Tail, Tail Fringe, Crest, Head, Eye Patch, Ruff

● DRAGON

1. From the reversible metallic gold fabric cut out one Left Body, one Right Body Top, one Lower Body, one Head, one Right Top Leg, one Right Bottom Leg, one Left Top Leg, one Left Bottom Leg and one Tail.

TIP: When using the double-sided fabric, flip selected pattern pieces to reverse them. The Body is cut in pieces to create a shaded effect by using the darker reverse side of the metallic fabric for some pieces. I cut the Right Body Top, Right Bottom Leg and Tail from the reversed fabric.

Option: You also can make the dragon all of one color fabric by assembling and cutting out the entire pattern as one piece except the Head, Ruff and Back Crests, but you probably will need to cut out the legs separately from the body, unless you find fabric that is wide enough.

2. From the red polyester cut one 4" x 27" strip, one 4" x 60" strip, and use the patterns in reverse to cut out one Head and one Ruff.

3. From the green metallic fabric, cut one 4" x 27" strip, one 4" x 60" strip and one Ruff.

4. From the black felt cut two eye patches.

5. On the red fabric Head, follow the pattern, and cut the horizontal slash as indicated.

6. From the batting cut one Head and one Ruff.

● QUILT

1. Evenly trim the selvage edges of the fleece.

2. Cut rounded corners on the fleece, using a 6" plate as a guide.

Serge edges.

Sew

● QUILT BACKGROUND

1. Finish the edges of the fleece with matching thread. Serge or overcast stitch the edges.

● BODY

1. Press a hem on the Left Body Top, along the Crest line.

2. Position the Right Body Top on the quilt.

3. Pin or fuse the Right Body Top in place.

4. Place the Left Body Top on the quilt, overlapping it ½" along the Crest line.

5. Pin or fuse the Left Body Top in place.

6. Position, then pin or fuse all four Dragon Legs in place.

7. Set the machine to wide zigzag with a short stitch length so the stitches are quite close together, yet not quite a satin stitch. Match the thread color to the Dragon pieces on top, and use bobbin thread that matches the quilt. Sew the pieces onto the quilt.

8. Re-sew any stitching that looks as if it might pull out.

TIP: To increase the stability of the woven Body fabric on the stretchy knitted fleece, you can topstitch 1" scalloped "scales" in rows across the entire dragon.

● CREST

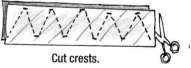

Cut crests.

Sew on crests.

1. Match one 4" x 27" strip of red fabric with one 4" x 27" strip of green fabric, right sides together.

2. Trace the zigzagging Crest design.

3. Sew fabrics together along the stitch line. Be sure to sew two or three stitches across the corners for easier turning.

4. Match one 4" x 60" strip of red fabric with one 4" x 60" strip of green fabric, right sides together.

5. Repeat Steps 2 and 3.

6. Trim away the extra crest fabric to make seam allowances ¼" from the seam line on the inside corner. Clip off the tops of the points.

7. Turn the crests. Press the crests flat. Pull the seam at the inside corners to smooth it.

8. Fold each Crest at the bottom of the points along the raw edge for the entire length. Press a hem.

9. Unfold the hem of the 27" Crest strip.

10. Align the pressed fold line to the seam along the spine between the Right and Left Body Tops, with the Crest positioned left of the seam line and the hem to the right.

TIP: Make short clips in the hem/seam allowance before pinning in place to ease it around curves.

---

11. Pin the Crest in place every few inches. Place pins across the stitch line for easy removal.

12. Topstitch on the Crest fold line and Body seam line from the Neck to the Tail. Remove pins.

13. Trim the Crest hem ⅛" from the stitch line from the neck to the tail. Make short clips to the seam line as needed to ease the Crest on curves.

14. Fold the Crest to the right to cover the stitch line. Zigzag stitch over this edge from Neck to Tail to secure the Crest in place and cover the raw edge.

15. Repeat Steps 6 through 14 to join the Crest to the Tail.

● RUFF

Make ruff.

Join ruff.

1. Pin the right sides of the green and red Ruff fabric pieces to the Ruff batting piece.

2. Sew around the layered edges. Leave the top end open to turn as marked. Be sure to sew the inside and outside corners with two or three stitches across for better turning.

3. Trim the seam allowances. Clip into the inside turns, and clip off the top of the points.

4. Turn the Ruff. Lay the finished Ruff right side up on the quilt back, at the Dragon's Neck.

5. Align the Ruff's open top edge with the quilt edge. Sew across Ruff and blanket raw edges to join the pieces.

6. Flip the Ruff back to the quilt front to hide the stitching. Pin the Ruff in place.

7. Topstitch quilting lines on the Ruff to join the pieces. Set the machine to a wide zigzag stitch with a short stitch length so the stitches are quite close together, yet not quite a satin stitch. Match the thread color to the Dragon pieces on top, and use thread that matches the quilt on the bobbin.

● HEAD

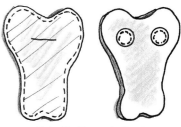

Make the Dragon's Head.

1. Iron paper-backed fusible web onto the back of the gold Head piece. Use the lowest heat setting possible.

2. Align the gold Head and red Head pieces, right sides together. Place the Head batting onto the fabric Head pieces.

3. Sew around the entire Head. Stitch through all three layers. Turn the Head right side out through the slit.

4. Position and sew the black Eye Patches in place.

5. Pin the Head onto the Ruff. Topstitch the Head and Ruff on the quilting lines to join the pieces.

Join the head to the quilt. Topstitch details. Glue on eyes.

Embellish

1. Quilt the nose lines onto the dragon.

2. Spread hot glue on the entire back of one plastic eye. Glue it in the middle of one black Eye Patch. Press the Eye firmly in place.

3. Repeat Steps 2 for the other Eye.

Wizard Cape

Materials

FABRIC
2 yd. silky purple polyester moon and stars print, 54" to 60" wide
2⅛ yd. solid purple polyester
⅓ yd. gold polyester satin

EMBELLISHMENTS AND NOTIONS
6" x 24" piece of quilting fiberfill
4" x 8" paper-backed fusible web
16" x 16" piece of stiff interfacing
4 gold 1" buttons
Threads in purple and gold

TOOLS AND SUPPLIES
Serger (optional)
Sewing machine
Needle
Sharp scissors
Pins
Iron and ironing board

This colorful coverlet serves as a light blanket, a wizard cape or even a tent.

This multiuse project reminded me of an art school friend who was a weaver. She wove a large, beautiful square of fabric that she used as a tablecloth. When she went out, she would sweep that weaving off the table and wrap it around her shoulders to wear as a shawl. I suspect that she was a neater eater than I.

To work out a cape design, I kept drawing and drawing various cape ideas, ones that could also serve as a quilt. They grew more and more complicated and less and less like a quilt. Finally I draped this wonderful polyester print fabric around my shoulders and tied two ends. Amazing! A cape!

Because the fabric is lightweight, silky and softly woven, it works well as a cape. A nice surprise was that the tighter I tied it using the stuffed stars, the shorter it became. It can fit anyone. Both my husband and my 7-year-old grandson have worn it.

Much of the charm of the cape is the fabric design. Many of these imaginative fabric designs show up in stores around Halloween, which now ranks right behind Christmas as a time to pull out all of the stops for fancy clothing. Keep an eye out for these seasonal fabrics that come in polyester, poly-cottons and mixes made into prints, sheers, nets and glittery designs for costumes and holiday clothing and decor.

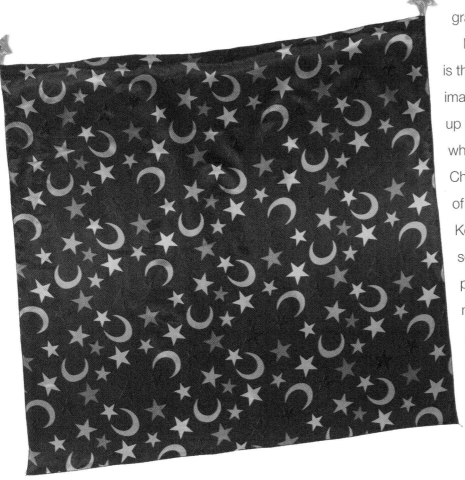

Cut

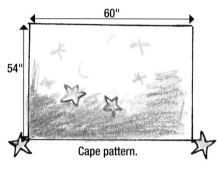

Cape pattern.

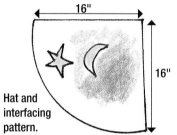

Hat and
interfacing
pattern.

1. From the moon and stars print fabric cut one 54" x 60" Cape.

2. From the purple polyester fabric cut one 54" x 60" Cape lining and one Hat.

3. From the gold satin fabric cut one Brim and four Stuffed Stars.

4. From the fiberfill cut one Brim.

5. From the interfacing cut one Hat.

Appliqué

1. Pin the interfacing to the Hat fabric. If the fabric is slippery, baste around the edges.

2. Trace one Moon and one Star onto the paper-backed fusible web.

3. Iron the fusible web onto the back of the fabric.

4. Cut out the fused Star and Moon.

5. Remove the paper backing from the fusible web.

6. Position the Moon and Star on the Hat. Iron them in place.

7. Satin stitch around each appliqué.

Sew

● **CAPE**

1. Place the Cape and Cape lining together, right sides out.

2. Align all of the edges of the Cape and lining.

3. Pin the Cape and Cape lining. If you plan to serge, position the pins 3" from the edge to keep them away from the cutter.

4. Sew around all four edges of the Cape and Lining using a rolled hem setting on a serger or an overcast stitch on a sewing matching. If you don't have a serger or good overcast stitch on your machine, align all the edges of the cape and lining, right sides together. Sew around the edges, leaving an opening to turn. Press the seam open, turn the fabric, and sew the opening closed with hidden hand stitches. Press again, and topstitch the edge if desired.

● **STUFFED STARS**

1. Align two Stuffed Stars, right sides together.

2. Sew the edges, leaving an opening to turn.

3. Turn the sewn Star. Lightly stuff the star.

4. Sew the opening closed.

5. Sew a gold button on each side of the Star in the center to quilt the star.

6. Repeat Steps 1 through 5 for the second Star.

7. Hand sew one Star securely to one corner.

8. Hand sew the other Star to the lengthwise corner. Make sure that the Stars are 60" apart.

● **HAT**

Fold fabric right sides together. Sew interlining and seam.

1. Fold the Hat, right sides together and interfacing outward. Align the straight edges with the fabric.

2. Sew the Hat from the top edge to the bottom.

Sew brim with interfacing filler.

3. Align the Brim to the bonded quilt batting.

4. Join the Brim fabric and layers every 2½" with straight and/or zigzag stitches in a contrasting color.

5. Fold the quilted Brim end to end, right sides together.

Stitch brim in circle shape.

6. Sew across the end of the Brim to make a loop.

7. Turn the Brim right-side out. Fold it back-to-back lengthwise.

Pull gathering threads to ease to fit.

8. Pin the Brim to the Hat's lower edge. It will need easing to fit. If you wish, run long basting stitches along the Brim. Pull stitches together the fabric to fit.

9. Serge or zigzag and trim the finished edge. Fold the brim upward 2" to conceal the stitching.

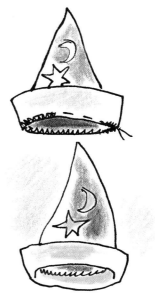

Finish the base of the hat.

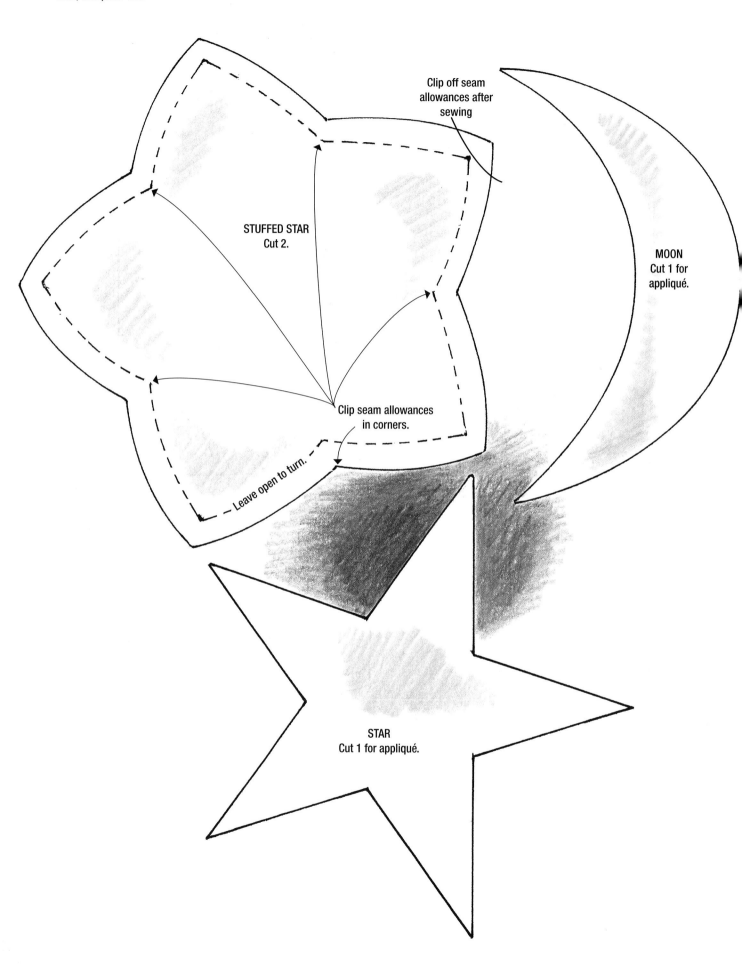

Clip off seam
allowances after
sewing

STUFFED STAR
Cut 2.

MOON
Cut 1 for
appliqué.

Clip seam allowances
in corners.

Leave open to turn.

STAR
Cut 1 for appliqué.

Game Quilts

Games are kids' "work" to develop their skills. These four quilts are
no exception, helping kids to master various skills while offering them fun
at the same time. Once the kids are worn out from all of these activities,
they can snuggle under these cozy quilts for nap time.

Maze Quilt

Materials

FABRIC
1½ yd. of 44" wide purple pre-quilted poly-cotton fabric

⅓ yd. of 42" wide blue, green and red poly-cotton print

¼ yd. of 60" wide off-white fleece

¼ yd. of 60" wide golden yellow fleece

⅛ yd. of 60" wide blue, green and purple print fleece

⅛ yd. of 60" wide pink print fleece

9" x 9" yellow poly-cotton print

6" x 8" scrap of pink felt

5" x 12" scrap of brown poly-cotton print

4" x 5" scrap brown poly-cotton print

3" x 4" scrap of dark gray fleece

1" x 1" scrap of green poly-cotton

FIBERFILL
Small bag of fiberfill stuffing

EMBELLISHMENTS
Two ¼" black buttons

Post and washer eye

NOTIONS
Threads in off-white, pink and lavender

Invisible thread

TOOLS AND SUPPLIES
Sharp scissors

Rotary cutter and cutting mat

Yardstick

Hand-sewing needle

Tailor's chalk or pencil

Pins

What's more fun and challenging to a kid than finding a way through the maze? This game draws on motor skills and spatial perception.

The maze here appears in the shape of a house. The little mouse in the attic must find his way to the kitchen after dark to sample that cheese, but he must sneak past the watchful cat. Go, mousie!

Don't have time or energy for an elaborate quilt? This one features some techniques for quick results. First, the quilt is made from a pre-quilted fabric with face fabric on both sides, so no layer quilting is needed. You may be a bit limited at the fabric store to what colors are available. Choose whichever you like best, and key the added colors to it. Or, make your own quilt layers with facing and backing fabrics over a batting layer.

The maze channels are lined with a fluffy fringe made from double strips of fleece. Use the grid created by the pre-quilted fabric as a guide for the house. Once you topstitch the appliques and other details in place, it's time to send the mouse on a mission for that midnight snack.

Cut

YOU WILL NEED THE FOLLOWING PATTERN PIECES: Door, Window, Windowsill, Mouse, Mouse Ear, Mouse Paw, Mouse Tail, Cheese, Cat, Cat Eye

1. From the purple pre-quilted fabric cut the 44" x 48" quilt background.

2. From the blue, green and red poly-cotton print cut 2" wide strips of fabric to total 5¼ yards for the quilt binding.

3. From the off-white fleece cut 1" wide strips that equal the following lengths and quantities: 28" (4); 16" (4); 12" (2); 8" (4); 4½" (2); 4" (10).

4. From the golden yellow fleece cut one Cheese and 1" wide strips that equal the following lengths and quantities: 12" (4); 8" (16); 4" (10).

5. From the blue, green and purple print fleece cut 1" wide strips that equal the following lengths and quantities: 28" (2).

6. From the pink print fleece cut one 3" x 4" rectangle for the chimney and 1" wide strips that equal the following lengths and quantities: 40" (2).

7. From the yellow poly-cotton print cut two Windows.

8. From the pink felt cut one Mouse, two Ears, two Paws and one Tail.

9. From the brown fabric cut one Door and two Windowsills.

10. From the brown poly-cotton print cut one 4" x 5" piece for the Mouse's house.

11. From the dark gray fleece cut one Cat.

12. From the green poly-cotton cut one Eye.

Measure and Mark

1. Following the diagram, measure and mark the house-shaped Maze path. Use tailor's chalk, pins or pencil to mark placements. All of the channels are 4" wide except the attic.

TIP: If you use pre-quilted fabric, you can use the quilted lines for placement. The fabric shown had squares that measured 2" across.

Appliqué

● WINDOWS

1. Fold in the raw edges on one Windowsill.

2. Appliqué the Windowsill across one Window.

3. Repeat Steps 1 and 2 for the second Window.

● CAT

1. Appliqué the Cat to one Window.

2. Position the green fabric Eye on the Cat. Appliqué with lavender thread.

3. Insert the post and washer eye.

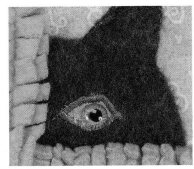

A post and washer eye adds detail to the cat.

● CHEESE

1. Follow the diagram and place the Cheese on the lower right corner of the quilt.

2. Appliqué the Cheese in place.

Sew

● BORDER

1. Sew the ends of the 2" wide Border strips together to make one long strip.

2. Match the Border edge to the quilt edge, right sides together. Pin

3. Position the Border edge around all sides of the quilt, leaving a ⅜" seam allowance. Pin the border in place. Leave an extra ½" at each corner.

4. Match the leftover Border ends. Sew across.

5. Trim off any extra fabric.

6. Sew the Border to the quilt, using a ⅜" a seam allowance.

7. Press a ½" hem on the Border.

8. Fold the Border over the quilt edge so the hemmed edge overlaps the seam line ⅛" on the backside.

9. Sew from the face side of the quilt. Stitch in the ditch (on the seam line) to finish the edge.

● DOOR AND WINDOWS

1. Place the Door on the quilt within the marked Maze channels.

2. Topstitch the Door around the edges, on the fringe seam line.

3. Repeat Steps 1 and 2 for the Windows.

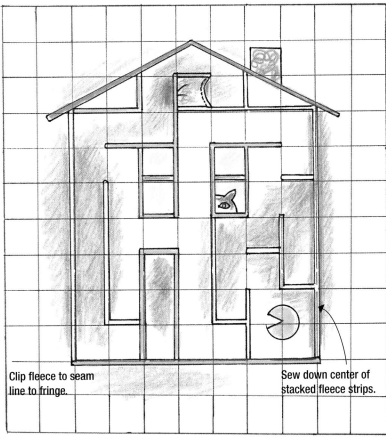

Clip fleece to seam line to fringe.

Sew down center of stacked fleece strips.

MAZE HOUSE PATTERN. Quilt is 44" x 48". Every square is 4".
Sew down center of doubled fleece strips. Clip to the seam line to create fringe.

● CHIMNEY

1. Place the base of the chimney on the roofline.

2. Trim the bottom edge of the chimney so it matches the angle of the roof and so the chimney runs parallel to the quilt edges.

3. Zigzag appliqué the chimney in place.

● MOUSE HOUSE

1. Fold over ⅜" on one of the 5" sides.

2. Topstitch a hem in the folded fabric.

3. Position the Mouse house fabric in its spot on the quilt. Make sure the hemmed side is the only one unbordered by a fleece fringe.

4. Tuck a fold in the unhemmed 5" side of the Mouse house fabric.

5. Topstitch the Mouse house in place on the three unhemmed sides. The folded area will create a gathered effect in the Mouse house once it is stitched.

● HOUSE OUTLINE

1. Stack the two 28" blue, green and purple fleece strips on top of each other, taking care to match the edges.

2. Center the strips over the bottom line of the house. Pin.

3. Topstitch through the center of the strips into the seam line, backstitching at both ends to secure. The sides of the strips will puff up.

4. Using sharp scissors, clip through both layers of fleece every ¼", snipping nearly to the topstitched line.

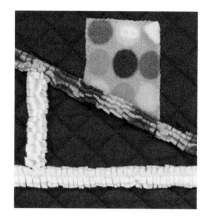

5. Repeat Steps 3 and 4 with 28" strips of off-white fleece, this time positioning the fleece to form the House sides.

6. Stack the two 40" strips of pink print fleece on top of each other, taking care to match the edges.

7. Place one end of the stacked pink print strips 3" to the left of the House wall. Angle 20" of the stacked strips up to the roof peak in the center of the quilt.

8. Angle the remaining 20" length of stacked strips down toward the right House wall to make a 3" eave past the right House wall. Pin the fleece to keep the roof angle in place long enough to sew it down.

9. Repeat Steps 3 and 4.

10. Follow the diagram to complete the maze. Position the strips, sew them in place, and cut the fringes.

● MOUSE

1. Fold the top of the Ear forward. Tuck it into the Ear Slot.

2. Sew across the Ear Slot.

3. Repeat Steps 1 and 2 for the other Ear.

4. Tuck the Tail in the Tail Slot.

5. Sew across the tail slot.

6. Fold the Mouse Body to align it.

7. Sew from the from the top of the Head past the Tail. Be sure to insert and include the Feet in this seam. Leave an opening large enough to stuff the toy.

8. Stuff the Mouse with fiberfill.

9. Sew the opening closed.

10. Sew the black button eyes onto the Mouse.

11. Add any embellishments as desired, such as black thread nostrils or a pink thread mouth.

The stuffed mouse toy adds a three-dimensional element to the project.

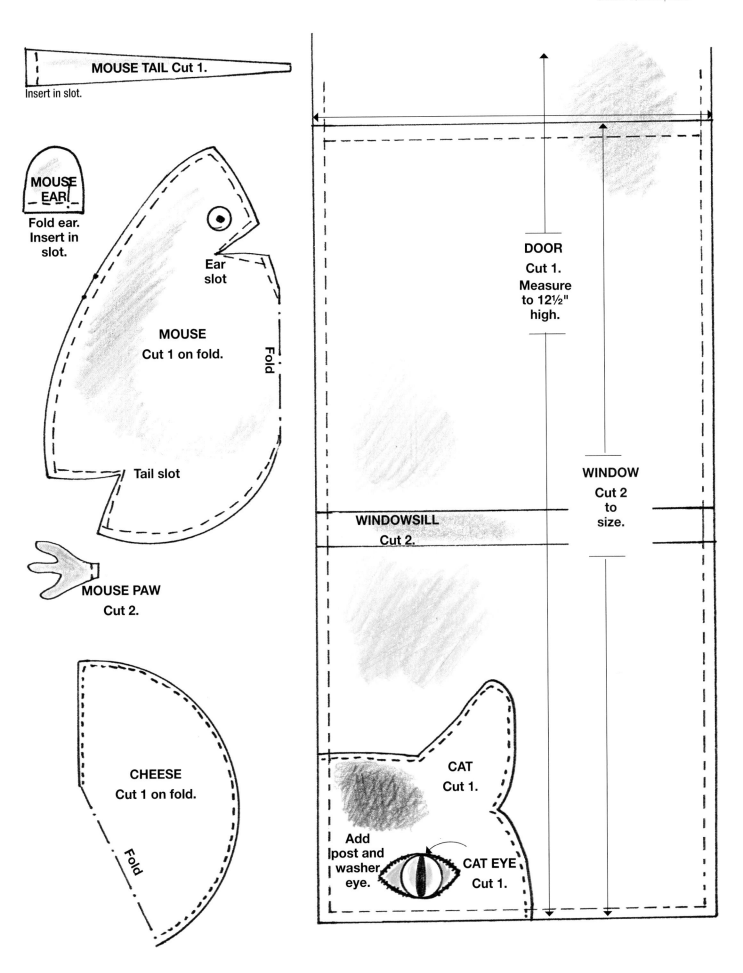

MOUSE TAIL Cut 1.

Insert in slot.

MOUSE EAR

Fold ear. Insert in slot.

Ear slot

MOUSE
Cut 1 on fold.

Fold

Tail slot

MOUSE PAW
Cut 2.

CHEESE
Cut 1 on fold.

Fold

DOOR
Cut 1.
Measure to 12½" high.

WINDOW
Cut 2 to size.

WINDOWSILL
Cut 2.

CAT
Cut 1.

Add post and washer eye.

CAT EYE
Cut 1.

Tic-Tac-Toe Game

Materials

Note: Unless otherwise noted, this project uses ½" seam allowances.

1⅔ yd. of 44" wide orange duck cloth or heavy poly-cotton

1 yd. of 44" wide red duck cloth or heavy poly-cotton

⅔ yd. of 44" wide green duck cloth or heavy poly-cotton

½ yd. of 44" wide black duck cloth or heavy poly-cotton

½ yd. of 44" wide bright yellow duck cloth or heavy poly-cotton

⅓ yd. of 44" wide white duck cloth or heavy poly-cotton

⅓ yd. of 44" wide pink duck cloth or heavy poly-cotton

⅓ yd. of 44" wide turquoise duck cloth or heavy poly-cotton

⅓ yd. of 44" wide purple duck cloth or heavy poly-cotton

¼ yd. of 44" wide gold duck cloth or heavy poly-cotton

¼ yd. of 44" wide magenta duck cloth or heavy poly-cotton

¼ yd. of 44" wide navy blue duck cloth or heavy poly-cotton

EMBELLISHMENTS AND NOTIONS

44" x 44" piece of bonded fiberfill batting (for quilt)

14" x 36" piece of bonded fiberfill batting (for X's and Os)

Threads in orange, purple, green and yellow

TOOLS AND SUPPLIES

Sharp scissors

Rotary cutter

Pins

Yardstick

Light and dark colored wax pencils

Sewing machine

Iron and ironing board

1 piece of cardboard, 8½" x 11"

Wax pencil

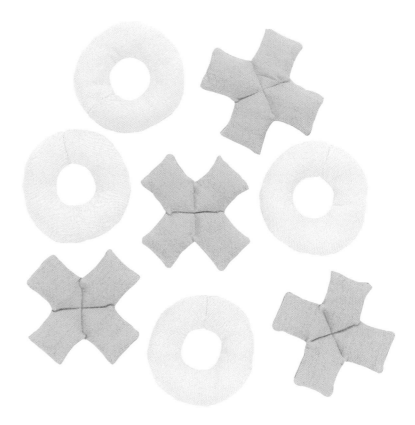

Tic-Tac-Toe usually is played with paper and pencil, or even with a stick in the sand, but here it is the basis for a quilt.

The stuffed X's and O's can store away in the colorful side pockets of the quilt. The heavy cotton canvas-like fabric is called duck cloth, which is stiff enough so that the game need not be quilted closely.

Called Noughts and Crosses on the other side of the Atlantic, Tic-Tac-Toe is probably the most common pencil and paper game around in the Western world. The rules are simple. Two players strive to get three symbols in a row on a nine-block grid. One player uses the symbol X, the other, O. The players take turns and put X's or O's in empty spaces in the grid.

The first to get three matching symbols in a row vertically, horizontally or diagonally wins. While a number of variations have sprung up, the main ones being 3-D Tic-Tac-Toe and 4 in a Row, the original game remains the best-known.

Cut

YOU WILL NEED THE FOLLOWING PATTERN PIECES: X pattern, O pattern

● FABRIC

1. From the black fabric cut nine 8" x 8" squares.

2. From the white fabric cut two 2½" x 26" strips and six 2½" x 8" strips.

3. From the green fabric cut two 2½" x 26" strips, four 2½" x 2½" squares and 10 X's.

4. From the red fabric cut two 2½" x 26" strips, four 8" x 8" squares, one 2½" x 8" strip, one 5" x 8" strip and two 8" x 42" strips.

5. From the orange fabric cut two 8" x 8" squares, one 2½" x 8" strip, one 5" x 8" strip, one 2½" x 42" strip and four 2½" x 2½" squares.

6. From the gold fabric cut two 8" x 8" squares, one 2½" x 8" strip and one 5" x 8" strip.

7. From the pink fabric cut two 8" x 8" squares, one 2½" x 8" strip, one 5" x 8" strip and one 2½" x 42" strip.

8. From the turquoise fabric cut two 8" x 8" squares, one 2½" x 8" strip, one 5" x 8" strip and one 2½" x 42" strip.

9. From the purple fabric cut two 8" x 8" squares, one 2½" x 8" strip, one 5" x 8" strip and one 2½" x 42" strip.

10. From the magenta fabric cut two 8" x 8" squares, one 2½" x 8" strip and one 5" x 8" strip.

11. From the navy blue fabric cut two 8" x 8" squares, one 2½" x 8" strip and one 5" x 8" strip.

12. From the yellow fabric cut 10 O's.

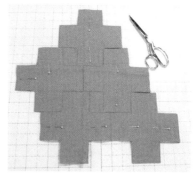

Try this layout to get the maximum number of X's from your fabric.

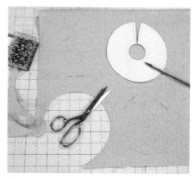

You can cut the O's on a double thickness of fabric.

● BATTING

1. From the 14" x 36" piece of batting cut five X's and five O's.

● CARDBOARD

1. From the cardboard cut one 1½" x 7" guide and one 7" x 7" square guide.

Trace

1. Use a wax pencil to trace the 7" x 7" square guide on the back of each square.

2. Use a yardstick to draw seam lines 1½" apart along each side of the long strips. (If you are a really accurate stitcher and you have cut all the pieces exactly, you may not need this step. I always measure and draw seam lines.)

Sew

TIP: Assemble the quilt from the center out, as you would a Log Cabin quilt. Refer to the diagram to ensure that you use each piece in its proper place. For a neat quilt, mark and match seam lines.

● GAME GRID

1. Pin one 2½" x 8" white strip to one 8" x 8" black square. Use ½" seam allowances. Repeat Step 1 five times.

TIP: Align the pieces and pin matching seam lines with pins at right angles to the line so you can sew over them by machine.

2. Stitch each pair of strips and squares to create six white strip/black square units.

3. Stitch two of the black/white units together to form a horizontal unit that follows the pattern of black/white/black/white.

4. Stitch one black square to the exposed white strip end. This completes the first row of the game grid.

5. Repeat Steps 2 through 4 to complete the remaining two rows of the game grid.

Lay out the pockets around the finished grid.

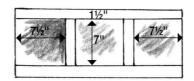

6. Press all of the seams open to the black side.

7. Sew one 2½" x 25" white strip to the bottom of one of the three black/white units and another to the top of the same unit.

8. On the back of the white strips, mark the seam lines across to match the added strips.

9. Press to the dark side of the fabric.

10. Align the seam lines on the white strip with the second black/white unit. Pin and sew.

11. Press to the dark side.

12. Match marks and seam lines and sew the black/white unit to the white strip on the other side. The white strips run horizontally between black/white units.

13. Press to the dark side.

● GRID BORDERS

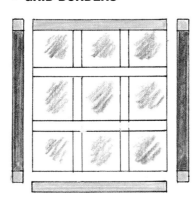

1. Align and sew one 2½" x 26" long green strip to the top and the

other 2½" x 26" long green strip to the bottom of the grid.

2. Sew a 2½" orange square to one end of the 2½" x 25" red strip.

3. Measure the red and orange strip against the completed green-strip bordered grid.

4. Sew the other orange square at the opposite end of the red strip so the total orange and red strip equals the length of the grid from green strip to green strip.

5. Repeat Steps 3 and 4 for the other 2½" x 25" red strip.

6. Position one red/orange/red strip on one side of the grid. Align seam lines on the orange corners and the green strip.

7. Stitch the red/orange/red strip to the grid.

8. Repeat Steps 6 and 7 for the other side of the grid.

● TOP FRAME

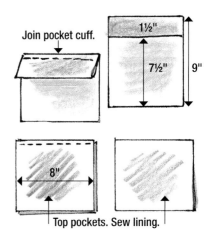

Join pocket cuff.

Top pockets. Sew lining.

1. Sew a 2½" x 8" magenta strip to one 8" x 8" gold square.

2. Sew one 2½" x 8" orange strip to one 8" x 8" red square.

3. Sew one 2½" x 8" gold strip to one 8" x 8" purple square.

4. Sew the orange strip to the gold square to create a row of magenta/gold/orange/red.

5. Sew the red square to the gold strip to expand the row to magenta/gold/orange/red/gold/purple.

6. Sew a navy strip to the purple square to create a strip that is magenta/gold/orange/red/gold/purple/navy.

7. Pin this strip to the top of the grid along the green border. Align seam lines.

8. Sew the magenta/gold/orange/red/gold/purple/navy strip to the green border.

● **BOTTOM FRAME**

1. Sew one 2½" x 8" purple strip to one 8" x 8" magenta square.

2. Sew one 2½" x 8" red strip to one 8" x 8" gold square.

3. Sew one 2½" x 8" turquoise strip to one 8" x 8" red square.

4. Begin connecting the two-color units by sewing the red strip to the magenta square. This creates a row of purple/magenta/red/gold.

5. Sew the turquoise strip to the gold square to create a row of purple/magenta/red/gold/turquoise/red.

6. Sew one 2½" x 8" pink strip to the red square to create a strip that follows the sequence of purple/magenta/red/gold/turquoise/red/pink.

7. Match seam lines and sew the completed purple/magenta/red/gold/turquoise/red/pink strip to the bottom of the grid along the orange/green/orange strip grid border.

● **SIDE POCKETS**

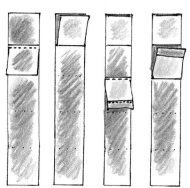

1. To make pocket cuffs, fold each of the eight colored 5" x 8" strips lengthwise. Press.

2. Mark a seam line so each folded strip measures 1½" wide from the fold to the line.

3. Sew each folded strip to a corresponding square in the following combinations:
  Left side:
    Pink strip/orange square;
    Navy strip/purple square;
    Orange strip/pink square; and
    Turquoise strip/navy square.
  Right side:
    Gold strip/pink square;
    Purple strip/orange square;
    Magenta strip/navy square; and
    Red strip/turquoise square.

4. Press the seam toward the square. Topstitch.

5. For the left top pocket, match one turquoise square and one red square, right sides together. The red square will form a pocket liner and the turquoise square will face out.

6. Sew along the top edge seam.

7. Turn, fold and press the seam. Topstitch in place.

8. On the backside of the lined square, mark a seam at 7½" along the bottom edge.

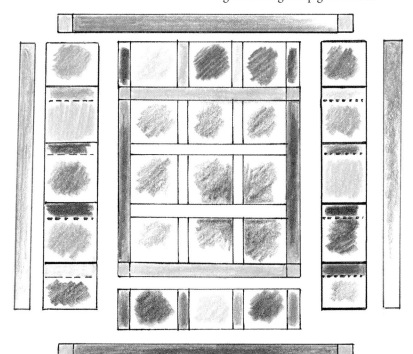

9. For the right top pocket, repeat Steps 5 through 8, this time pairing a magenta square with a red pocket liner square.

● POCKET STRIP

1. Starting at the top of the backside of one 8" x 44" red pocket strip, mark seams across the 8" width at the following measurements: 7½" down from the top; 16" from the top; 24½" from the top; and 33½" from the top.

2. Repeat Step 1 for the other red pocket strip.

3. Lay the turquoise pocket, right side down on the front. Match the seam mark on the red strip back. The pocket top on the red strip back should point downward, and the pocket seam allowance should point upward.

4. Pin through both marks from front to back to align seam lines. Place pins across the seam lines.

5. Sew the turquoise pocket in place on the pocket backing. Flip the pocket upward and pin in place.

6. Lay the orange pocket square with the pink cuff right side down on the red strip front, over the second backing seam mark. The pocket top should point down and seam allowance point up. Pin.

7. Sew the orange pocket along the seam mark. Flip the pocket up to meet the bottom edge of the turquoise pocket.

8. Match, pin, sew and flip the purple and pink pockets to the third and fourth seam marks respectively, using the techniques in Steps 6 and 7.

9. Position the navy pocket at the bottom of the strip. Pin it to the backing. The edge sashing will cover this seam.

10. Repeat Steps 3 through 9 to complete the other strip of side pockets, which will run in order from top to bottom as magenta, pink, orange, purple and turquoise.

11. Draw a seam line on the red pocket backing. Align the red pocket backing with the assembled grid and edging, carefully matching seam lines and strips.

12. Sew a seam to join the pocket backing and the grid.

13. Repeat Steps 11 and 12 for the second set of side pockets.

● BORDER STRIP

1. Draw seam lines on the four 2½" x 42" border strips so the strips measure 1½" across, seam to seam, with ½" seam allowances on each side.

2. Align the 2½" x 42" orange border strip with the bottom edge of the bottom assembled frame. Match the seam lines and sew.

3. Align the 2½" x 42" pink border strip to with the top edge of the frame. Match the seam lines and sew, but avoid stitching the top side pockets shut.

4. Align the turquoise and purple border strips with the left and right sides, respectively, of the side pocket strips. Adjust the strips to align with the top and bottom seam lines.

5. Sew a green 2½" x 2½" square at each end of the purple and turquoise strips.

6. Align the green/turquoise/ green strip on the left side of the quilt. Match seam lines and sew.

7. Align the green/purple/green strips on the right side of the quilt. Match seam lines and sew.

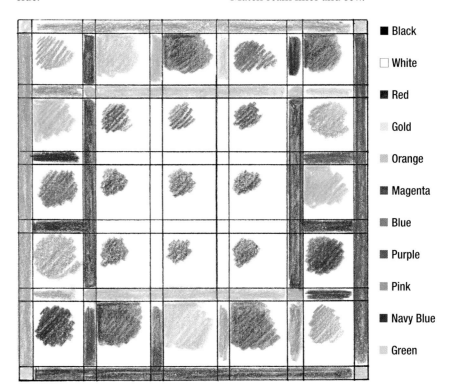

- ■ Black
- □ White
- ■ Red
- Gold
- Orange
- ■ Magenta
- ■ Blue
- ■ Purple
- Pink
- ■ Navy Blue
- Green

● BACKING

1. Lay the assembled quilt face up on a flat surface.

2. Lay the orange backing fabric on top of the quilt face and smooth it out.

3. Pin the backing and quilt face around the edge, matching seam lines.

4. Sew the backing and quilt face together, leaving a 9" opening at the center bottom to turn.

5. Sew three short stitches across each corner diagonally.

6. Lay the quilt flat, grid side up. Spread and smooth the 44" x 44" piece of bonded fiberfill batting over it.

7. Trim off the extra batting.

8. Pin the batting in place. Re-sew the edge seam from the backing side.

9. Clip across the corner to grade the seam.

10. Turn the quilt right side out. Push the corners out to square them out.

11. Sew the opening closed by hand or machine.

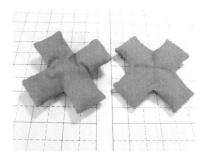

Quilt

1. Lay the quilt out on a flat surface and smooth it flat.

2. Pin the quilt in several places to anchor the layers.

3. Machine or hand sew to quilt the seams. Stitch in the ditch (sew on the stitch line so stitches don't show), but be careful to avoid stitching the pocket top into the seam. Use a matching thread on the bobbin and one of the color threads on the top.

TIP: I tried to use a transparent thread, but it kept breaking over the thick seams, so a purple thread, a middle-value color, looked OK.

● X'S

1. Match two X's, right sides together.

2. Sew around the perimeter using a ¼" seam allowance.

3. Angle a stitch across the inside corners. You can reverse stitch here, as well, to reinforce the corner. Leave one end of the X open to turn and stuff.

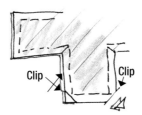

4. Clip into each inside corner to the stitch line so it will not pull on the seam when turned.

5. Clip across the outside corners to avoid lumps.

6. Turn the X right side out. Poke out the outside corners with a turning tool.

Stuff. Tuck in edges. Sew shut.

7. Stuff the X lightly.

8. Tuck in the seam allowance. Hand sew the X closed with a hidden stitch. Or machine sew across the end with an exposed seam.

9. Repeat Steps 1 through 8 for the four remaining X's.

● O'S

1. Match two O's, right sides together.

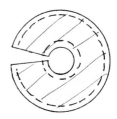

2. Use a ¼" seam allowance and sew the O's around the inside and outside perimeters.

3. Leave both ends of the circle open.

4. Clip into the seam allowance, up to the seam line, in several places inside the circle. The fabric will pull enough to bring the circle

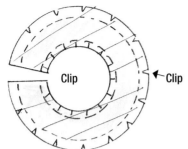

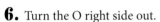

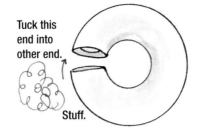

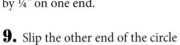

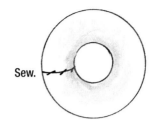

5. If you used a heavy fabric, clip little notches in the outside seam allowance.

6. Turn the O right side out.

7. Stuff the O lightly.

8. Fold the seam allowance under by ¼" on one end.

9. Slip the other end of the circle into the tucked end by ¼".

10. Match the seams. Hand Sew around the O to finish.

11. Repeat steps 1 through 10 for the four remaining O's.

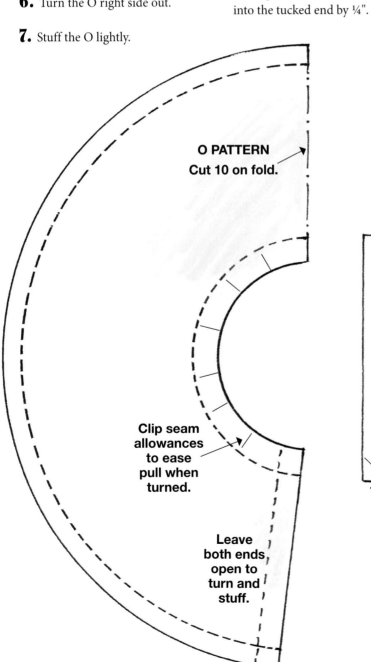

O PATTERN
Cut 10 on fold.

Clip seam allowances to ease pull when turned.

Leave both ends open to turn and stuff.

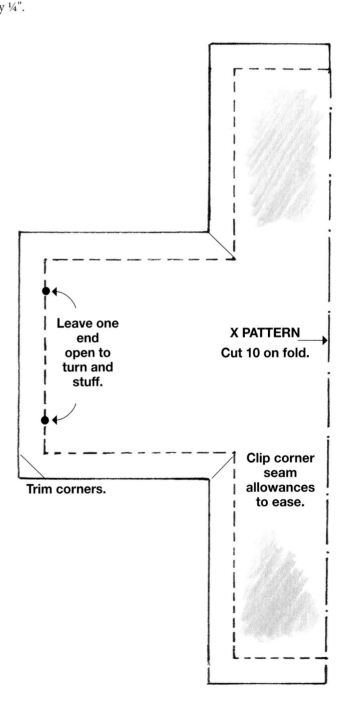

Leave one end open to turn and stuff.

X PATTERN
Cut 10 on fold.

Trim corners.

Clip corner seam allowances to ease.

Target Quilt

Materials

FABRIC
2 yd. 60" wide royal blue fleece
1 yd. 60" wide orange fleece
½ yd. 60" wide white fleece
½ yd. 60" wide yellow fleece
¼ yd. gold fleece
¼ yd. lime green fleece
¼ yd. light blue fleece
12" x 12" scrap of red fleece

FILLING
Bag of polystyrene pellets

NOTIONS
Threads in red, lime green, yellow, gold, light blue, orange and white
Tear-away stabilizer
Hook and loop tape (optional)

TOOLS AND SUPPLIES
Sewing machine
Serger (optional)
Hand sewing needle
Sharp scissors
Yardstick
Pushpins
Corkboard or tape
String
Quilting pins
Paper
Pencil

Kids banished to their rooms at nap time can entertain themselves with this quilt. The target design comes from the sport of archery, but it uses soft bags instead of arrows.

Just toss the beanbags onto the target to see if you can hit the bull's eye. Older kids can compute their scores and make up rules or variations, like tossing the beanbags with their eyes shut, over their shoulders or with their toes.

There's a rod pocket in the top so the quilt can be hung on the wall to see how good your aim really is. If you want the beanbags to stick in place, sew the stiff hook side of hook and loop tape patches on them so that they will stick for a bit.

How to Make a Full-Circle Pattern

Materials

24" length of string

Pushpin

Scissors

Pencil

Paper measuring 37" x 37"

Corkboard or another porous surface to hold the pushpin in place

Optional: Tape or additional pushpins to hold the paper in place during tracing.

1. Position a piece of paper that is 37" x 37" on a porous surface. If you're using a vertical surface, you may need to tape or pin the paper in place.

2. Insert one pushpin through the exact center of the paper.

3. Cut a 24" length of string.

4. Tie a loop knot in each end of the string so it measures 18½".

5. Loop one end around the pushpin, which will stay anchored in the center of the paper until you are done drawing circles.

6. Position the pencil tip in the other loop end of the string.

7. Hold the string taut, and draw a 37" circle.

8. Shorten the pencil-loop end of the string so it measures 15".

9. Keep the string taut and draw a 30" circle.

10. Shorten the string again so it measures 11½".

11. Keep the string taut and draw a 23" circle.

12. Shorten the string again so it measures 8".

13. Keep the string taut and draw a 16" circle.

14. Shorten the string again so it measures 4½".

Cut

● PATTERNS

1. Copy and cut out the 0, 1, 3, 5, 7, Pocket, Beanbag and Beanbag Dot patterns from the book.

2. Pull out the Target Ring pattern from the back of this book.

Note: The Ring Patterns provided are one-quarter segments of the finished circles they will create. You can flip the patterns as needed during tracing to get the ring and circle sizes you need, or you can make your own full-size pattern of the concentric circles used in this quilt with the directions at left.

● FABRIC

1. From the royal blue fleece cut the quilt background. If you are using a serger to finish the edges, cut a piece that measures 44" x 70". If you are hemming the edges with a sewing machine, cut a piece that measures 46" x 74" to allow for a 1" hem on all the sides of the quilt.

Note: The finished quilt will measure 44" x 66"; the additional length is to accommodate rod pockets at the top and bottom of the quilt.

2. From the orange fleece cut two 7's and one 36" diameter ring. Cut the ring in two semicircles.

46"

3. From the white fleece cut two 1's and one 16" diameter circle.

4. From the yellow fleece cut two 5's and one 30" diameter ring. Cut the ring in two semicircles.

5. From the gold fleece cut one Pocket and two Beanbags.

6. From the lime green fleece cut two Pockets and two Beanbag Dots.

7. From the light blue fleece cut two 3's, one 0, one 1, one Pocket and two Beanbags.

8. From the red fleece cut two Beanbag Dots and one 9" diameter circle.

Sew

● QUILT BACKGROUND

1. Trim the selvages from the quilt background material.

2. Finish the quilt background. Either serge along all four edges of the fleece or turn under a 1" hem and topstitch the hem in place.

3. Fold over a 2" hem at the top and at the bottom edges of the quilt background.

4. Topstitch the hem, leaving the ends open so a rod can slide into the slot for hanging.

● BEANBAGS

1. Follow the pattern to appliqué the Beanbag Dot on the right side of the unsewn Beanbag.

2. Fold the Beanbag fabric in half widthwise, placing right sides together. Or fold the Beanbags, backsides together, leaving the raw edges exposed.

3. Sew the Beanbag. Leave an opening to pour in the pellets.

4. If needed, turn the Beanbag right side out.

5. Fill the Beanbag with pellets.

6. Hand stitch the Beanbag opening shut.

● TARGET RINGS

1. Join the two orange Target Ring segments together to create a full ring.

2. Stitch the ring segments together with hidden hand stitching. The Target numbers will go over this seam so it won't show.

3. Repeat Steps 1 and 2 for the yellow Target Ring.

● TARGET

1. Fold the quilt in half lengthwise, then widthwise, to find the center.

2. Position the white circle in the center of the quilt. Pin it in place.

3. Position the red Bull's Eye in the center of the white circle. Pin. Sew.

4. Position the yellow ring 3½" from the white ring. Pin. The blue fabric between the white circle and yellow ring will serve as another ring for the target. If needed, you can use the Target Ring Pattern to position the yellow ring.

5. Position the orange ring outside the yellow ring. Pin it in place.

6. Baste the rings in place. Fleece is very flexible and fuzzy, so basting keeps it in position while machine sewing it.

7. Machine sew each ring in place with a double row of topstitching. Sew the first row ⅛" from the ring edge. Sew the second row ½" from the first.

● POCKETS

1. Sew a hook patch on the pocket lining. Position it down 1" from the top, and center it.

2. Match a lime green Pocket lining with a gold Pocket, placing right sides of the fabric together.

3. Use a ¼" seam allowance to sew the around three sides of the pocket, leaving a 3" opening in the center on one side. This makes all four corners sewn the same.

4. Clip the corner seam allowances and turn the pocket right-side out.

5. Topstitch the pocket top edge in place, ¼" from the edge. Tuck in the side seam opening to sandwich the raw edges.

6. Position the finished pocket, lime green side down, on the bottom right corner of the quilt. The bottom outer edge of the pocket should be 3½" in from the side of the quilt and 3½" up from the bottom of the quilt. Align the Pocket loop patch with the hook patch. Sew in place.

7. Topstitch the pocket in place, ¼" from the edges.

8. Repeat Steps 1 through 7 with the light blue and lime green fleece pieces.

Appliqué

● NUMBERS

TIP: You can appliqué the numbers either before or after you attach the rings to the quilt. I did it after; doing it before may be easier because you won't have as many thicknesses of fabrics.

1. Position the corresponding number. Center it over the seam(s) of its ring or on the vertical center line.

2. Position tear-away stabilizer behind the number and ring.

3. Pin the layers.

4. Baste the number in place. Otherwise, it will shift and distort.

5. Sew around the number using a long zigzag or satin stitch. You also can hand stitch the numbers in place. Tear away the stabilizer.

6. Repeat Steps 1 through 5 for all of the numbers on the target rings.

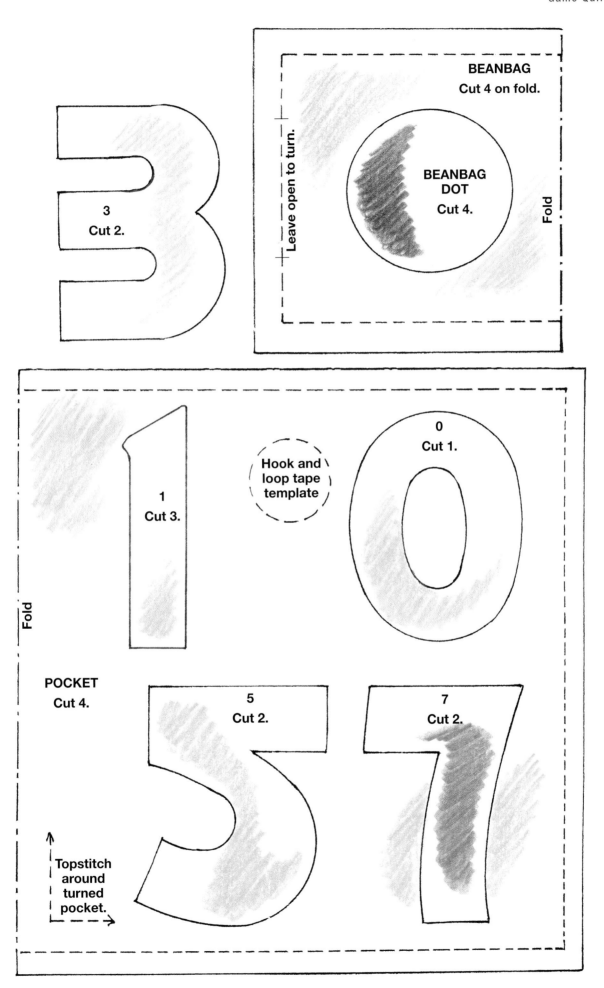

3
Cut 2.

BEANBAG
Cut 4 on fold.

Leave open to turn.

BEANBAG DOT
Cut 4.

Fold

1
Cut 3.

Hook and loop tape template

0
Cut 1.

Fold

POCKET
Cut 4.

5
Cut 2.

7
Cut 2.

Topstitch around turned pocket.

Hopscotch Quilt

Materials

FABRIC
1⅓ yd. 60" wide tan fleece
½ yd. 60" wide red fleece
⅓ yd. 60" wide sky blue fleece
½ yd. 60" wide lavender fleece
½ yd. 60" wide purple fleece
⅓ yd. 60" wide yellow fleece
½ yd. 60" wide dark green fleece
⅓ yd. 60" wide gold fleece
⅓ yd. 60" wide orange fleece
⅓ yd. 60" wide white fleece

NOTIONS
Threads in purple and tan

TOOLS AND SUPPLIES
Sharp scissors or rotary cutter and cutting mat
Quilting pins
Fabric tape (optional)
18" straight-edge ruler
Chalk pencil

Hopscotch is an age-old game usually played with chalk on a sidewalk or paved street. Each player selects a pebble or coin, then tosses it on the squares. The player must then hop over any square with a pebble on it; the first player to make it all the way up to eight and back to the start wins.

This fleece quilt project offers a softer, more portable version of the game, but it will rumple and slide on a smooth floor. It's safest to put this quilt on the rug for a hopscotch contest.

Fleece comes in an ever-increasing variety of colors and patterns. Some fleece is nonpilling, some quite fluffy, and some even is one-sided, such as the blue fleece I used in this project.

To make the quilt without lining, use double-sided fleece. For this, sew the seams with a three-needle serger and pull the seams flat, which will expose stitching. Better yet, overcast and topstitch for a flat fell seam by regular machine.

You also can use other fabrics, such as poly-cotton broadcloth or duck cloth. For thinner quilting fabrics, add fiberfill batting and a backing as you would for a traditional layered quilt, then machine quilt in the ditch along seam lines.

The finished size of this quilt measures 46" x 52", but since it is based on a grid, you easily could make it a different size if you wish.

Cut

YOU WILL NEED THE FOLLOWING PATTERN PIECES: 1, 2, 3, 4, 5, 6, 7, 8

Note: A narrow hem of ¼" is included for serging. If you plan to machine sew, add ¼" to each side for ½" seams.

1. From the tan fleece cut a 46" x 52" backing.

2. From the red fleece cut two 9" x 9" blocks; one 9" x 18" block; and one 3" x 52" strip for the side border.

3. From the sky blue fleece cut two 9" x 18" blocks.

4. From the lavender fleece cut two 9" x 18" blocks and two 3" x 47" border strips.

5. From the purple fleece cut two 9" x 18" blocks and the numbers 1, 2, 3, 4, 5, 6, 7 and 8.

6. From the yellow fleece cut two 9" x 9" blocks.

7. From the dark green fleece cut two 9" x 9" blocks, one 9" x 18" block and one 3" x 52" border strip.

8. From the gold fleece cut two 9" x 13½" blocks.

9. From the orange fleece cut one 9" x 9" block and one 9" x 13½" block.

10. From the white fleece cut one 9" x 9" block and one 9" x 13½" block.

Appliqué

1. Position the Number 1 in the center of the 9" x 9" yellow square, making sure the number is 2" away from the top and bottom edges.

2. Pin or tape the number in place.

3. Zigzag stitch around the number to applique. If the number shifts as you sew, straight stitch the edges first to secure it.

4. Repeat Steps 1 through 3 for the remaining seven numbers, making sure to match the number with the correct color block.

Sew

● QUILT TOP

Note: If you sew by serger, place any pins at least 2" from the edge to be sewn to avoid breaking the cutting blade on a pin. Make sure the top fleece does not slide on the lower piece to begin stitching.

1. Lay out the quilt pieces in order on a table or floor to ensure that your colors look good and that all of the pieces fit.

2. Construct the quilt by joining the blocks in three- and four-block horizontal rows. For Row 1 (the bottom row), join the right side of block A to the left side of block B, then the right side of block B to the left side of block C.

3. Repeat Step 2 for Rows 2 through 6.

4. Match the seams on Row 1 with Row 2.

5. Sew Rows 1 and 2.

6. Match the seams of Rows 2 and 3.

7. Sew Rows 2 and 3. You now will have a three-row segment.

8. Fold Row 5 in half to locate its center point.

9. Match the center seam of Row 6 with the center of Row 5.

10. Sew Rows 5 and 6 together.

11. Match the center of Row Five to the center seam of Row Four.

12. Sew Rows 4 and 5. You now will have another three-row segment.

13. Match the center of Row 3 to the center seam of Row 4.

14. Sew Rows 3 and 4, which will connect the two three-row segments into a single six-row piece.

● BORDERS

1. Lay the quilt top flat and align one side red border on the quilt edge.

2. Pin the Border in place. Stitch.

3. Repeat Steps 1 and 2 for the other side.

4. With the quilt laid flat, align the top Border across the sixth row and Border ends.

5. Pin the top Border in place and sew.

● BACKING

1. Lay the backing flat on a large table or the floor and smooth it out.

2. Place the assembled quilt top, right side down, on the backing.

3. Match the edges of the quilt top and backing, and trim off any extra backing.

4. Pin the quilt top and backing together. Place pins every 6" along the edges across the stitch line for machine sewing, or 2" in from the edge for serging.

5. Begin 9" in from one corner and sew all around the quilt edges, taking care to round all four corners. Be sure to leave a 12" opening to turn the quilt and clip off the corner seam allowances for sewing machine sewn seams.

6. Turn the quilt and poke out the corners.

7. Use hidden stitches to hand sew the opening closed.

8. Machine or hand quilt the layers together. Stitch in the ditch on the horizontal seams and around the border. Sew quilting stitches in the seam to hide them.

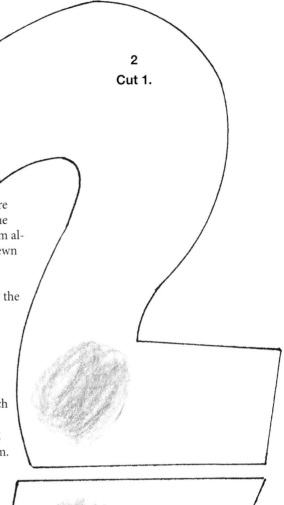

2
Cut 1.

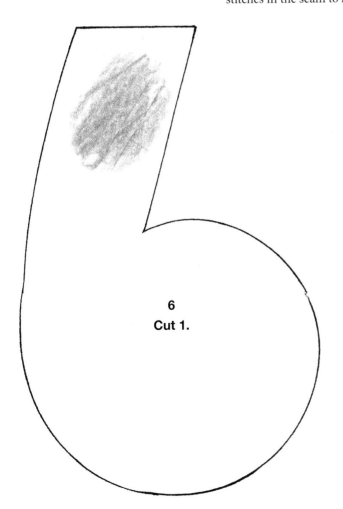

6
Cut 1.

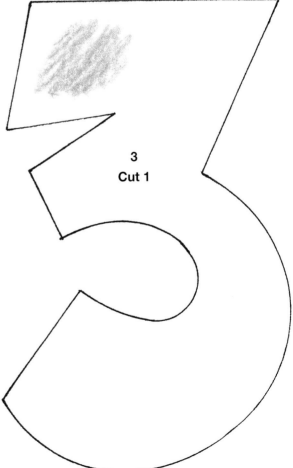

3
Cut 1

4
Cut 1.

5
Cut 1.

7
Cut 1.

1
Cut 1.

8
Cut 1.

Do-It Quilts

Busy fingers and lively imaginations will find hours of fun with these quilts.

Children can work at length learning to button and unbutton with the butterflies and flowers on the Flower Button Quilt. Learning how to work buttons can be difficult, so be sure to sew the buttons on firmly. Secret things appeal to kids, and two of these projects offer secrets of their own. The batik Dog Pillow hides a stuffed puppy pal; just unfold the hem to let him out. The Egg Quilt/Pillow has a surprise, too, as the quilt can tuck up inside the egg shape to form a pillow. Children can travel as far as their imaginations will reach with the Bumper Car Quilt. The quilt is an adaptation of one of favorite childhood activities.

Flower Button Quilt

Materials

FABRIC

1¼ yd. of 60" wide green print fleece fabric

2 pieces of 8" x 12" white felt

2 pieces of 8" x 12" yellow felt

8" x 12" piece of 8" x 12" black felt

8" x 12" piece of l8" x 12" ight pink felt

8" x 12" piece of bright pink

8" x 12" piece of light blue felt

8" x 12" piece of purple felt

8" x 12" piece of bright orange felt

8" x 12" piece of light orange felt

8" x 12" piece of red felt

FUSIBLE WEB

1 yd. paper-backed fusible web (optional)

NOTIONS

50 buttons, 1" in diameter

Threads in green, light orange, brown, white and pink

Four spools of thread to match with the projects (optional)

TOOLS AND SUPPLIES

Serger or sewing machine

Hand sewing needle

Sharp scissors

Sharp, soft pencil

Paper (optional, for creating your own patterns)

Iron and ironing board

Right angle glide (optional)

Maybe the germ of the idea for this quilt began long ago when my kids were little.

Back then I'd say, "Nap time. I don't care what you do in your rooms for an hour, but I need a nap." And they went. (They weren't the kind to destroy the place.)

With something like the Flower Button Quilt, the kids could have rearranged the flowers, butterflies and bees on this quilt endlessly, buttoned other things onto the quilt or buttoned the flowers, butterflies and bees onto pieces of clothing. After all, they had a whole hour at a time to experiment.

The quilt is easy to make by hand or machine. The basic fleece quilt measures 37" x 45", although it can be any size you choose up to the 60" width of fleece. You can sew the buttons on by sewing machine if all the buttons have exposed holes. Shank buttons will require hand sewing.

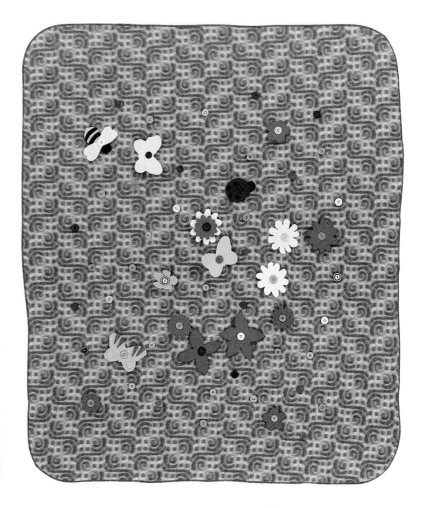

Cut

YOU WILL NEED THE FOLLOWING PATTERN PIECES: Bee Wings, Bee Body, Bee Stripes, Butterfly, Daisy, Impatiens, Lily, Zinnia. Feel free to design your own button-on patterns, such as ladybugs or maple leaves.

1. Trim the selvages from the green patterned fleece.

2. From the green patterned fleece cut the quilt background to the desired size. The quilt shown is 37" x 45".

TIP: Use a right angle guide or the edge of a table to make straight edges and squared corners. Be careful: Fleece fabric shifts.

3. Trace and cut various flowers, bees, butterflies or other patterns for the quilt. Choose the patterns that best suit your tastes.

4. Clip a ¾" buttonhole in the center of each piece to be buttoned on to the quilt, as shown on the pattern.

TIP: For increased sturdiness, you can sew the buttonhole edges by machine or by hand. You also can use thread to embellish the added pieces.

Appliqué

1. For the Bee, iron paper-backed fusible web on to the back of each Bee Stripe.

2. Peel off the paper backing.

3. Iron each Bee Stripe onto the Bee Body.

TIP: To make the flowers, bees and butterflies stiffer, cut them out double, iron paper-backed fusible web on the back of one, peel off the paper and iron the first piece onto another matching piece.

Sew

● QUILT

1. Set the serger, or use the sewing machine to create an overcast stitch. Use the serger's variable feed to make an edge without ripples.

2. Sew or serge around the entire edge of the quilt to create a finished edge.

● BUTTONS

1. Place the buttons randomly on the quilt, making sure they are several inches in from the edge and at least 4" to 5" apart so the felt patterns do not overlap.

Secure the knot.

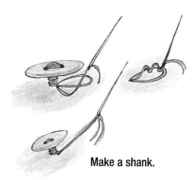

Make a shank.

2. Add the buttons. To sew the buttons on by hand, use a sturdy thread that is doubled and knotted at the end. Sew a ⅛" stitch into the quilt. Sew back through the double threads at the knot to secure the button.

3. Sew back through the holes several times. Pull tightly.

4. Wrap the thread around the threads under the button two or three to make a shank.

5. Sew a tiny stitch at the shank base. Leave a short loop.

6. Put the needle through the loop twice to make a knot and pull tightly. Repeat for a double knot.

7. Clip off the thread ¼" from the knot.

TIP: To sew the buttons on by machine, set the stitch width to match the buttonholes, hold the button securely, and sew.

8. Button the finished flowers, bees and butterflies onto the buttons.

IMPATIENS
Buttonhole

BUTTERFLY
Buttonhole

BEE BODY

BEE STRIPES
Cut black stripes.

Cut whole body of yellow.

BEE WINGS
Buttonhole

DAISY
Buttonhole

ZINNIA
Buttonhole

LILY
Buttonhole

Cut pieces out of a single layer of felt, or cut
out double pieces that you fuse together.

Egg Quilt and Pillow

Materials

FABRIC
1⅔ yd. of Easter egg print fleece, or print of your choice

½ yd. eggshell-colored fleece

¼ yd. pink spotted fleece

4½" x 15" scrap of coordinating patterned fabric

NOTIONS
15" length of pink hook and loop tape

1½ yd. of bias tape to match fleece

Threads in peach and cream

TOOLS AND SUPPLIES
Serger or sewing machine

Sharp scissors

Pins

Yardstick

Pencil

Paper for templates

Just as an egg hatches, a pillow can turn into a quilt, or quilt into a pillow. When the quilt is spread on the bed, you'll notice that there's a large egg appliquéd on it. Surprise! The egg has a hook and loop tape closure under a decorative stripe. Open the egg, stuff the entire blanket inside, adjust it a bit to fit smoothly, then close the hook and loop tape, and you have an egg pillow.

The pillow shown is shaped like an egg, but it could as easily be a football, basketball, apple, fat banana or similar plump shape of the same size. This will be influenced in part by what pattern of fleece you can find. I found this delightful Easter egg quilt last year. The finished quilt is 55" x 60," but you can make it the size you wish. Just remember that a larger quilt will need a larger egg (football, or whatever) to fit inside.

Cut

YOU WILL NEED THE FOLLOWING PATTERN PIECES: Egg Quilt Top, Egg Quilt Bottom, Top Narrow Strip, Bottom Narrow Strip, Medium Strip, Wide Strip

● PATTERN PIECES

1. Cut out the Egg Quilt Top and Egg Quilt Bottom from the pattern insert in the back of the book.

2. Using the Egg Quilt Top and Egg Quilt Bottom pieces, trace and cut out templates for the Top Narrow Strip, Bottom Narrow Strip, Medium Strip and Wide Strip. (The Front Strip will cover the hook and loop tape.)

● FABRIC

1. Spread the Easter egg print fleece out flat, and use a yardstick to trim all the selvage edges from the fleece.

2. Cut the Easter egg print fleece to the finished 55" x 60" size of the quilt background.

3. From the eggshell colored fleece cut one Egg Top and one Egg Bottom.

4. From the pink spotted fleece cut one Top Narrow Strip, one Bottom Narrow Strip and one Medium Strip.

5. From the patterned fabric cut one Wide Strip.

Sew

● QUILT BACKGROUND

1. Use the serger or an overcast stitch on the sewing machine to finish the edges of the Easter egg print fleece. Or, hand sew the edges using a buttonhole stitch.

● EGG

1. Pin the Wide Strip in place on the back side of the Egg Top.

2. Use a zigzag stitch to sew the Wide Strip in place. Use matching thread on the bobbin.

Note: The sheer, flimsy fabric used for this stripe needed a hem to keep from fraying. Topstitched lines it held it more securely. Judge what your fabric needs.

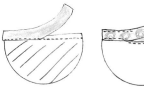

3. Align the hook side of the hook and loop tape with the top edge of the tape, overlapping the straight bottom edge of the Egg Top by ½", as well as the side opposite from the Wide Strip. Pin the ends to keep the fleece from stretching. Do not stretch the fleece to fit, or the hook and loop tape will ripple.

4. Sew the tape in place on the Egg Top.

5. Position the Top Narrow Strip so it covers the raw edge of the Wide Strip and conceals the back side of the hook and loop tape. Pin in place.

6. Zigzag across the edges of the Top Narrow Strip.

7. Match the back side of the Egg Bottom with the back of the loop side of the hook and loop tape. Pin in place.

8. Sew the loop side of the hook and loop tape in place.

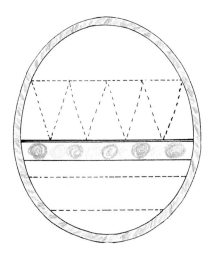

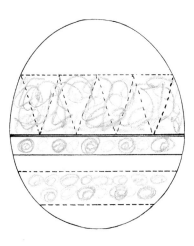

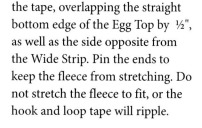

● **EMBELLISH**

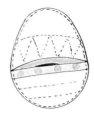 

1. Sew the bias tape over the seam where the Egg and quilt background are joined. You can sew the tape either by hand or machine.

Option: Cut fabric strips on the bias to create your own binding.

9. Align the edge of the Bottom Narrow Strip with the edge of the hook and loop tape so the strip covers the tape. The hook and loop tape will face the same side as the wide strip on the Egg Top.

10. Zigzag stitch the Bottom Narrow Strip to the Egg Bottom.

11. Position the Medium Strip on the back side of the Egg Bottom. It will be on the same side as the loops for the hook and loop tape.

12. Zigzag stitch the Medium Strip in place.

13. Join the hook and loop tape strips together to join the egg halves.

14. Position the joined Egg Top and Egg Bottom on the quilt as shown.

15. Sew the Egg Top and Egg Bottom in place, straight stitching ¼" from the edge.

Note: Fleece has high loft and is stretchy. This makes sewing close to the edge difficult. Use either the correct sewing machine foot or keep tucking the fleece out of the groove in the foot.

Bumper Car Quilt

Materials

FABRIC

2 yd. red fleece, 40" wide

1½ yd. red satin, 19" wide

6" x 12" scrap of silver fabric

FILLING AND FUSER

6" x 12" piece of paper-backed fusible web

18" x 18" foam pad, 1" thick

NOTIONS

Thread in red, and silver or gray

TOOLS AND SUPPLIES

Scissors

Serger

Iron and ironing board

Sewing machine

Yardstick

1½" quilting pins

When my sister and I were kids, we often made our own toys. One rambunctious game we enjoyed involved stacking a pillow on a blanket at the top of the polished oak stairs. The "driver" would sit on the pillow, pull the blanket up over her feet and go bumping down the stairs, toboggan style.

This car quilt is a modern-day version of that old game that my grandchildren still play. With this project, more modern fabrics replace the pillow and blanket. Fleece, which is soft and stretchy, is ideal for the top surface of this "pull-on" car. The slippery satin bottom surface helps the car slide down the stairs best. However, satin does not stretch. This means to join these two fabrics, you'll need to pin the satin to the fleece before stitching to ensure the fleece does not stretch.

The silver fabric used for the headlights may be fragile, so I've suggested fusing it. This also stabilizes it for quilting and appliqué stitches. Experts suggest avoiding heat fusers with fragile metallic fabrics and fuzzy fleeces because those fabrics may melt or matt. To get around this, fuse the headlights on from the back side of the satin to reduce the heat load.

Cut

YOU WILL NEED THE FOLLOWING PATTERN PIECE: Headlight

1. Cut the selvage off of the red fleece so it measures 38" x 72".

2. From the red satin cut one 19" x 54" piece.

3. From the paper-backed fusible web, cut two Headlights.

4. From the silver fabric cut out two Headlights.

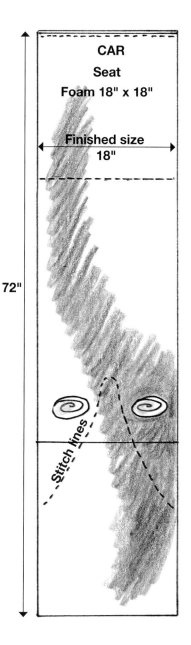

CAR

Seat

Foam 18" x 18"

Finished size 18"

72"

Stitch lines

Applique

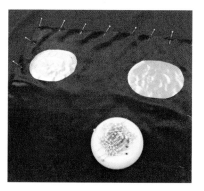

1. Place the paper-backed fusible web Headlights on the reverse side of the silver fabric.

2. Iron the fusible web onto the back of the silver fabric. Peel the paper backing off of the fusible web.

3. Position each headlight 3½" from the top edge of the satin and 1" in from each side, then pin in place.

4. Flip the satin over and iron fabric from the backside to fuse. Use care to avoid overheating the fabrics.

5. Straight or free-motion stitch a row of spiral stitches from the edge to center of each headlight.
   Note: Secure the fabrics firmly in place. Regular play, as well as wear and tear, will result in a lot of tugging on the fabrics.

Sew

1. Spread out the fleece.

2. Press a ½" hem under on the left and top edges of the satin.

3. Lay the satin, right side up, on top of the fleece. Match the edges from the lower right corner.

4. Align the raw edges of the fleece and satin on the right and bottom edges.

5. Pin the fabrics every 4" along the side and bottom edges. This will help stabilize the fabric and prevent sliding and stretching before stitching. Place pins across the seam line, on the left hem of the satin and across the top edge of the satin.

6. Zigzag stitch the satin to the fleece up the left edge.

7. Straight stitch the top, right side and bottom edges of the fabrics.

8. Fold the fleece and satin inward vertically, and match the raw edges. Serge or sew across the bottom fleece/satin/fleece raw edge.

9. Turn the corner and sew up the side, enclosing the satin in this seam.

10. Turn the Car right side out.

11. Finger press and pin the satin edges flat.

12. With red thread on the bobbin and silver/gray thread on top, satin stitch around the Headlights. This quilts them as well.

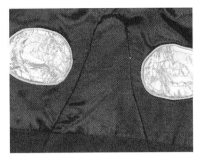

13. Topstitch the car hood line from each side down to the center between the headlights and back up to the side to quilt it as shown.

14. Straight stitch across the Car, 20" from the open end.

15. Fold the foam cushion and push it into the top open end of the car. Unfold.

16. Smooth the surface, and flatten the cushion.

17. Above the cushion, fold a ½" hem in the raw edges. Hem or serge across to finish.

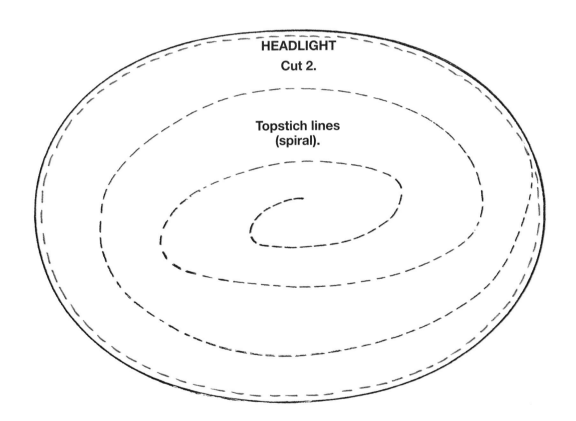

HEADLIGHT
Cut 2.

Topstich lines (spiral).

Dog Pillow

Materials

FABRIC

⅔ yd. green batik print fabric

½ yd. of ⅜" pile black and white spotted faux fur

⅓ yd. orange fleece

8" x 12" scrap of black wool or flat-weave black fabric

8" x 12" scrap of black faux fur

6" x 6" scrap of taupe velveteen

FIBERFILL

12 oz. fiberfill stuffing

NOTIONS

Thread in black and green

EMBELLISHMENTS

Two 22 mm plastic post and washer eyes

TOOLS AND SUPPLIES

Sewing machine

Sharp scissors

Quilting pins, 1½" long

Black permanent marker (optional)

Black squeeze paint (optional)

Chalk

It's fun to have a secret pal. This project appears to be an ordinary pillow, but when it's opened, out pops a Dalmatian dog. You can make any kind of pet —dog, cat, bear or mouse —by altering the fur, the color and the ears. The entire pillow can be washable, depending on the fabrics you choose.

Cut

YOU WILL NEED THE FOLLOWING PATTERN PIECES: Dog Head Front, Dog Head Back, Foot, Paw, Nose, Ear

1. From the black and white faux fur cut one Dog Head Front, one Dog Head Back and four Feet. Mark Eye, Nose and Paw placement.

TIP: When cutting out the faux fur pieces, mark the pattern on the reverse side of the faux fur fabric and slide scissors tips through the pile to avoid trimming the pile.

2. From the black faux fur cut out two Ears (one reversed) and one Nose.

3. From the black fabric cut out two Ears (one reversed).

4. From the taupe velveteen cut two Paws.

5. From the orange fleece cut an 11" x 26" rectangle for the pillow cuff.

6. From the batik print fabric cut a 22" x 26" rectangle for the pillow cover.

Sew

● NOSE

TIP: If flying fibers from faux fur bother you, wear a pollen mask while sewing.

1. Pin the Nose in place and sew basting stitches around it.

2. Satin stitch the Nose with black thread to outline and secure.

3. Turn the Head over to sew the Nose-to-Neck dart.

● MOUTH

1. Satin stitch from the Nose to the Mouth.

2. Satin stitch the mouth or use squeeze paint for the mouth.

● EYES

1. Clip or punch a small hole in the faux fur for each Eye post.

2. Insert the Eye posts. Push each corresponding washer onto the post as firmly as possible. Some plastic eyes may have a screw-on post and nut.

● EARS

1. Pair one faux fur Ear with an Ear lining, placing pieces right sides together.

2. Seam the Ear and Ear lining. Leave an opening at the base to turn the Ear.

3. Clip the seam allowances. Turn the completed Ear right side out.

4. Repeat Steps 1 through 3 for the other ear.
  Note: The softer lining allows the Ear to flop forward.

● FEET

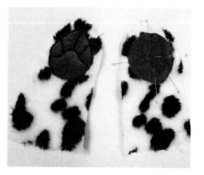

1. Pin a Paw on each Foot front.

2. Baste each Paw in place.

3. Satin stitch the edges of each paw, then satin stitch to outline the toes and Foot pad. Underlying fur will puff the quilted Paws.

4. Join a front and back Foot, right sides together, and sew the edges. Leave the straight end open to turn the piece right side out. As you sew, brush the fur out of the seam with your fingers or a long pin.

5. Turn the Foot. Pick the fur pile out of the seam by running a pin or scissors tip across the fur.

6. Repeat Steps 1 through 5 for the other Foot.

7. Stuff the Paws on each Foot with fiberfill. Baste across the open ends of the Feet.

● HEAD

1. Align and pin the Ears as marked to the top of the Head Front, with the Ear linings facing the Head fur so the Ears flop forward. Either pin across the stitch line or baste the Ears to the Head Front.

2. Align the Head Front and Head Back, right sides together. Keep the Ears tucked out of the seam.

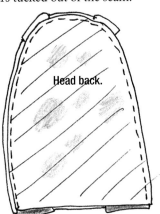

Head back.

3. Sew the Head Front and Head Back together, leaving the bottom open to turn. Turn the Head right side out.

4. Align the Foot to the raw edge of the Head front as marked. Baste.

5. Repeat Step 4 for the other Foot.

● PILLOW

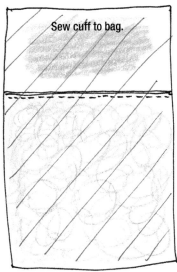

Sew cuff to bag.

1. Pin or baste the 26" side of the pillow cuff to top of the 26" side of the pillow cover. Pin or baste carefully. The fleece stretches, but the fabric does not.

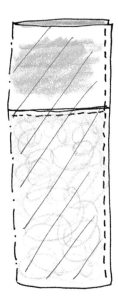

2. Sew across this seam.

3. Fold the pillow, right sides together. Match the cuff raw edges, align the cuff/pillow seam exactly, and match the pillow edges.

4. Sew the cuff and pillow, leaving both the top and bottom ends of the pillow open.

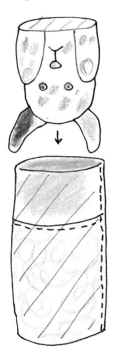

5. Slide the Dog Head into the fleece cuff. Align the raw edges of the Dog Head bottom edge with the cuff/pillow seam. Pin and sew this seam.

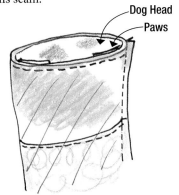

Dog Head

Paws

6. Turn the pillow right side out to the Cuff seam. With the Cuff inside, begin to fold the pillow back down over itself.

Cuff seam

7. Fold the pillow downward, face-to-face over itself, until the folded edge aligns with the Head/Cuff joining seam. Pin.

8. To sew the seam, use a long zigzag stitch to catch the edge of the fold and Cuff/Dog edges.

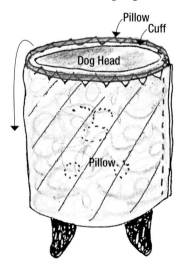

Pillow
Cuff
Dog Head
Pillow

9. Turn the pillow right size out. When opened, only zigzag tacking stitches will show.

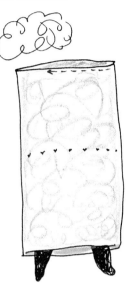

10. Stuff the Head. Stuff the pillow. Use lofty stuffing and stuff just enough to keep the shape.

11. Tuck a hem in the bottom edge of the pillow.

12. Sew the pillow closed with machine or hidden hand stitching.

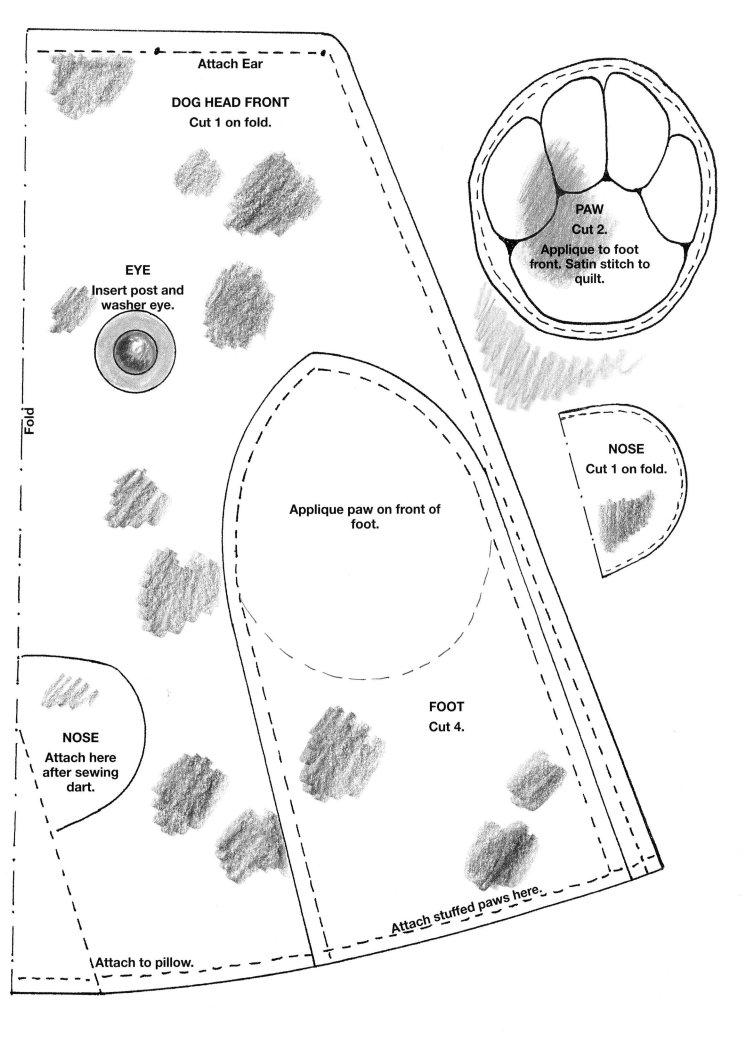

Attach Ear

DOG HEAD FRONT
Cut 1 on fold.

PAW
Cut 2.
Applique to foot front. Satin stitch to quilt.

EYE
Insert post and washer eye.

Fold

NOSE
Cut 1 on fold.

Applique paw on front of foot.

NOSE
Attach here after sewing dart.

FOOT
Cut 4.

Attach stuffed paws here.

Attach to pillow.

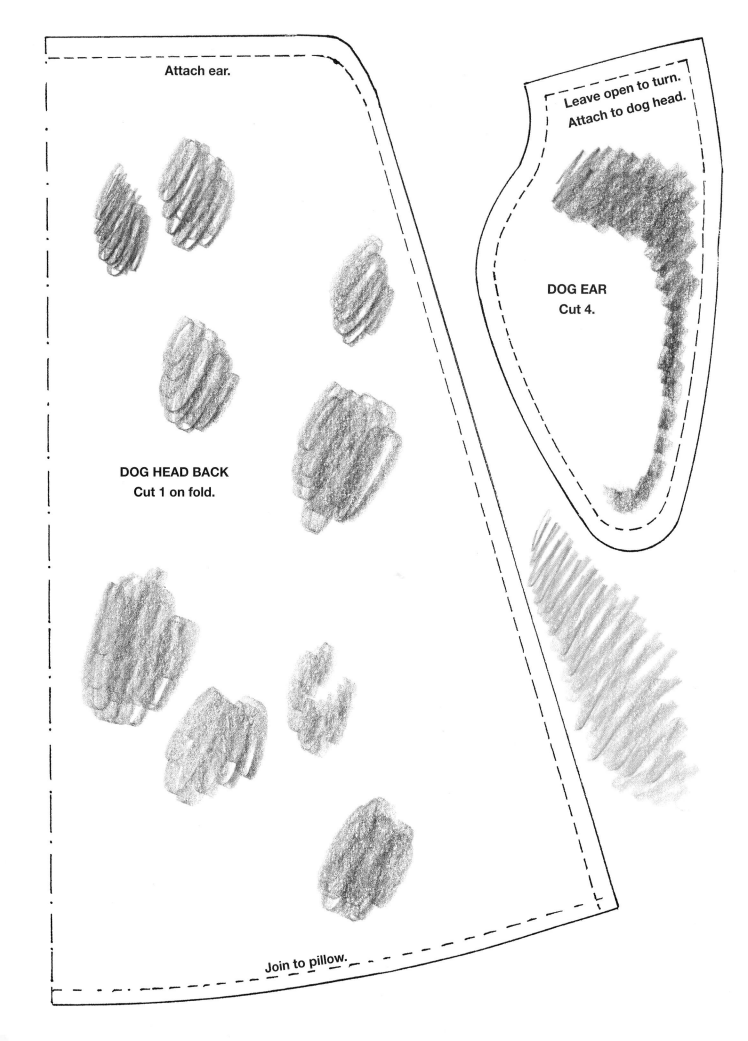

Attach ear.

Leave open to turn.
Attach to dog head.

DOG EAR
Cut 4.

DOG HEAD BACK
Cut 1 on fold.

Join to pillow.